THE LETTERS OF
PAUL

With a Preface by
JOHN SHELBY SPONG
EPISCOPAL BISHOP OF NEWARK

D0188364

RIVERHEAD BOOKS, NEW YORK

Riverhead Books
Published by The Berkley Publishing Group
A member of Penguin Putnam Inc.
200 Madison Avenue
New York, New York 10016

Preface copyright © 1998 by Bishop John Shelby Spong
Book design by Tiffany Kukec
Cover design by Charles Björklund
Cover art: El Greco (1541–1614), *Saints Peter and Paul*,
Hermitage, St. Petersburg, Russia/Scala/Art Resource, NY

First Riverhead edition: August 1998

The Penguin Putnam Inc. World Wide Web site address is
http://www.penguinputnam.com

Library of Congress Cataloging-in-Publication Data

Bible. N.T. Epistles of Paul. English. Authorized. 1998.
The letters of Paul / with a preface by John Shelby Spong.—1st
Riverhead ed.
p.   cm.—(Riverhead sacred text series)
Includes bibliographical references.
ISBN 1-57322-683-1 (trade paper)
I. Title.   II. Series.
BS2890.A3.   1998
227'.052032—dc21   98-18588
CIP

Printed in the United States of America

10 9 8 7 6 5 4 3 2 1

CONTENTS

CONTENTS

PREFACE

*An External and Internal Introduction to Paul,
the Architect of Christianity*

Paul was born in Tarsus, the capital of the Province of Cilicia in what came to be known as Asia Minor. His date of birth appears to have been no earlier than 6 B.C.E. and no later than 15 C.E., with the weight of the evidence pointing toward the earlier year. He appears to have died in Rome probably somewhere between 63 C.E. and 67 C.E. So his life span was 59 years at the shortest estimate and 74 years at the longest. Once again the weight of evidence would point to the probability that Paul was around 70 years of age when his earthly pilgrimage came to an end.

He was the son of Jewish parents who had Roman citizenship. Scholars are not certain how they came to acquire this citizenship, but there seems to be little reason to doubt Luke's suggestion that Paul was born into this status, as a part of his inheritance from his parents.

When we look into the history of the city of Tarsus, we discover that it was absorbed into the Roman Empire in 66 B.C.E. and that it played various roles in the struggle for political power among the competing factions that sought to rule the Empire—opposing Cassius, for example, who had murdered Julius Caesar, the patron of Tarsus. For that opposition Cassius imposed huge taxes on the city and proceeded to collect them ruthlessly.[1] However, as the political wheel of fortune turned again with the rise to power of Mark Antony in 41 B.C.E., the city was rewarded for that same opposition.[2] Mark Antony granted Tarsus both freedom and immunity from taxation.[3] This rare privilege was renewed in 31 B.C.E. after the battle of Actium by Augustus, who also conferred upon Tarsus land, laws, honor and the power to control the river and the sea in that part of the world.[4] These things, according to the practice of the Empire, were frequently accompanied by the gift of Roman citizenship to significant members of the population. We do know that between 18 B.C.E. and 14 C.E. the number of Roman citizens in this city increased by almost a million.[5] Perhaps this is how Paul's parents came to receive the citizenship that they passed on to their son, who appears to have claimed his Roman connection proudly.

Despite its Roman status, Tarsus was still more an oriental city than a western city, at least in its dress and in its taste for music.[6] Its roots went back to the Empire of the Hittites in the third millennium B.C.E.[7] In the first century it was a well-governed, relatively prosperous city with a kind of Hellenic respect for education and with the ability to equip its own citizens to face both East and West and to function competently in both worlds. Paul would be the beneficiary of that heritage.

In addition to being Roman citizens, Paul's family also appears to have been well-to-do. He certainly received educational opportunities generally not open to the poor. Paul's attitude toward physical labor, expressed in his letters to the Corinthians (1 Cor. 4:12, 9:19, 2 Cor. 11:7), suggests that he was among the economic elite and had little or no experience working as a laborer with his own hands.

The family in which Paul was raised, according to an abundance of biblical hints, was strictly observant of its Jewish heritage. Paul's passion for the traditions of Judaism surely reflected the value system that he learned in his home. Paul has said of himself that he was "circumcised on the eighth day." He also described himself as a "pharisee" in terms of the law and as "blameless" in terms of righteousness (Phil. 3:4–6). It would be quite unlikely that he would have acquired this level of commitment to the faith of his fathers and mothers had he not been born into a family that valued this faith and practiced it with devotion. Certainly there was in Tarsus a synagogue with a Hebrew school associated with it. This school, I suspect, was an important part of the young Paul's life. There was also the custom among the dispersed but faithful Jews of the Empire that two drachmas would be paid annually by every male for the support of the Temple in Jerusalem. One would imagine that Paul's family made that contribution with enthusiasm. The Jewish people of the diaspora never ceased to be citizens of two worlds, one being the world of the nation in which they were physically domiciled and the other being the world of their spiritual home, which was centered in Jerusalem and specifically in the Temple.

Paul was a citizen of the first century who straddled the Jewish world and the Mediterranean world. It is fair to say that he, like all of us, was shaped by the cultural attitudes of his time. There is no such thing as a universal human being. There is only a particular life residing in a particular moment of history who accepts the values and definitions of his or her era and processes reality through the knowledge available in that period of history. That should surprise no one except those who act as if the words of a particular man are to be equated with the words of God and thus to ascribe to those words both external and infallible truth. Unfortunately, throughout Christian history that fate has befallen Paul's words more than once. So let me be quite clear: Paul did not write the words of God. He wrote the words of Paul. His words were sometimes inspired words, sometimes insightful words and sometimes even visionary words. One has only to look at the hymn to the power and meaning of love in 1 Corinthians 13 to find an eloquent example. But Paul also wrote words that are seldom, if ever, quoted because they reveal his anger, his ignorance, or his prejudice. One could cite as an example a passage in Galatians (5:12) where he said, "I wish those who unsettle you would mutilate themselves," or in Romans (11.8) when he expressed his negative judgment toward some members of his own Jewish nation, "God gave them [the Jews] a spirit of stupor, eyes that should not see and ears that should not hear, down to this very day."

So to read Paul accurately one must read him as he was, a limited citizen of his century whose life was marked by moments of great spiritual power and by moments of an embarrassingly petty humanity. Paul accepted uncritically, for example, the patriarchal value system of his day that regarded men as created in God's image and women as a lesser creation, who should be subject to their husbands (Col. 3:18). He also asserted that it was "shameful" if women spoke in church (1 Cor. 14:35). As a child of his time he accepted slavery as a legitimate social and economic institution and contented himself to urge only that it be a kinder and gentler form of slavery (Philem., Col. 3:22ff). Furthermore, he appears to have accepted the Levitical definition of homosexuality found in the holiness code (Lev. 18, 20) as evil and worthy of judgment (Rom. 1:18–32). Each of these attitudes was present inside the prevailing definitions of Paul's day, and each was part of the pattern of cultural assumptions out of which Paul operated. Those who read Paul today need to appreciate these realities and seek to understand Paul's genius in terms of the limits of his day and his world. No one can finally transcend the time in which he or she lives.

Paul's parents, according to Luke in the Book of Acts, gave to their son the Hebrew name of Saul. It was a name with a double meaning. Paul stated that he was a member of the tribe of Benjamin (Phil. 3:5). In that tribe the name Saul had a special history. Saul, the son of Kish, of the tribe of Benjamin, had been chosen to be the first king of the Jewish nation (1 Sam. 9). He had been selected for this role, according to the biblical text, because of his imposing physical characteristics. Not only was he handsome, but "from his shoulders upward he was taller than any of the people" (1 Sam. 9:2). Jewish history, according to the biblical story, did not, however, paint King Saul heroically. Indeed, he was portrayed as a melancholy, tragic figure whose depression had to be soothed with music and who flew into rages that revealed the probability of mental illness (1 Sam. 16:14–23). He also lost the political support of the prophet Samuel, who according to the sacred story, had been the kingmaker in the first place. So Saul's royal line was not to be established. Its end was precipitated when Samuel, claiming to be acting for God, sought out, found and anointed a replacement. His choice was a young man not from among the sons of the tribe of Benjamin, but rather from the tribe of Judah, whose name was David (1 Sam. 16:6–13). This act set into motion the inevitable conflict over the ownership of the royal line, which David finally won. Yet the name "Saul" was still honored among the people of Israel and most especially among the people of the tribe of Benjamin for whom it always projected an impressive image. Perhaps that influenced Paul's parents who, as Benjaminites, decided to make Saul their son's Hebrew name.

There was, however, another side to this name, apparent in the Greek-speaking world, that made it somewhat difficult. The Greek language had the word *saulos*, an adjective, that carried with it the connotation of effeminacy. It is perhaps because of this connotation that when the Hebrew name "Saul" was written in Greek, it almost always became either Silas or Silvanus, never Saul.[8] Nothing is more common among schoolboys than to make fun of a classmate's name if they can find a way to do so. Paul seemed to have an awareness of the habit of making puns on people's names.[9] Perhaps that came from his own childhood as a victim of this experience.

Unfortunately, Paul's physical appearance seemed to make him more susceptible to the "saulos" connotation of his name than to the King Saul image. Though we cannot be absolutely certain of Paul's physical characteristics, there are hints that his stature and demeanor were not kinglike. From Paul's own writings we find one descriptive verse in which he has repeated a critic's charge in order to refute it. His enemies had said of him, "His letters are weighty and strong, but his bodily presence is weak and his speech is of no account (2 Cor. 10:10)." It is interesting to note that Paul's defense against this charge consisted of his refutation of only half of that criticism. Paul wrote, "Even if I am unskilled in speaking, I am not in knowledge" (2 Cor. 11:6). It is not too large a leap to suggest that he made no defense against the other half of this charge because he knew well enough that a powerful bodily presence he was not.

This autobiographical hint was reinforced by Luke in the Book of Acts, when he related a story of how the people of Lystra mistook Barnabas and Paul for gods. Barnabas, who appeared to be an imposing physical presence, was identified with Zeus, the king of the gods, while Paul was identified with Hermes, the messenger god (Acts 14:1–18).

Hermes was normally depicted in that society as a small, wiry, fast and verbal deity. Though this does not constitute a strong proof in our quest to be able to envision this central New Testament character, it does add a bit to the increasing possibility that this sense of physical smallness was an accurate portrayal of Paul of Tarsus.

A third confirming source can be found in a late second-century document entitled "The Acts of Paul and Thecla." There we find the first overt description of Paul from a human physical point of view. In that text he is called small in stature, bald-headed, bowlegged, vigorous, with meeting eyebrows and a slightly hooked nose.[10]

Alone this source would not be definitive since it came so late, but it does suggest that no attempt had been made to transform Paul's physical characteristics to correspond to his enhanced stature in the Christian community of that day, so that it rings with some authenticity. It also continues the ongoing impression that Paul's stature did not constitute a dominating impression. Indeed, he might well have been susceptible to having the name "saulos" applied to him in a mean, but not unheard of, way. Perhaps that is why the suggestion has been made that Paul used his Jewish name only among Jews, where the connotations of the Greek adjective "saulos" were not present, but he used the name Paul when he was among Greek-speaking Gentiles. There is also the suggestion that his family, who would need to give their son both a Jewish name and a Roman name, chose Paul because it came closest in their minds to the Hebrew name Saul.

We still must note, to be certain that it is registered, that nowhere in the Pauline corpus does Paul ever use any name but Paul. The suggestion that his name was also Saul comes to us exclusively from the writings of Luke in the Book of Acts (see chapter 9). But no indication can be found that Luke had any motive in this matter except to relate a fact that he knew to be true, and so we assume, I think with high levels of confidence, that Saul among Jews and Paul among Gentiles were in fact the names by which this person was known.

Paul clearly benefitted from the superior school system in Tarsus. He was not only fluent in Greek, but he also wrote the language with the flair of one whose education was extensive. In addition to Hellenic schools, he was also trained in the Hebrew school associated with the local synagogue, since for Jewish families religious education was obligatory through age twelve. He knew both Hebrew and the Torah, though he appears to have read the Hebrew scriptures primarily in the Greek version we call the Septuagint. His letters reveal no less than ninety citations from the Septuagint.[11] He appears to have mastered oratorical skills, which were considered to be the key to advancement in his world. Oratory, in his day, was based on letter writing and the study of speeches. The letters would actually be written as speeches designed to be read aloud to a public assembly.[12] The form of communication called epistles, for which Paul is known, was clearly born in this practice and reflects this style. Paul even indicates that he expects his letters to be used in this manner (2 Cor. 13:4–12). Though Paul liked to denigrate his speaking ability (1 Cor. 1:17, 2:4), the fact remained that his writing style was powerful.

Paul, following the custom among the upper classes of Tarsus, was sent abroad to complete his educational process. That is what brought him to Jerusalem at some point prior to the twentieth year of his life. The estimates are that he was in Jerusalem for about fifteen years before his conversion to Christianity, crucial years in Paul's life and development. His unusual zeal for the traditions of his father[s] enabled Paul to reach rare heights of excellence as a student. He was acclaimed and praised by his superiors. His dedication to keeping his religious traditions pure appears to have been the force that led him into the stance of a persecutor of the liberalizing Jewish Christian minority. Because it is inevitable that one draws near to that which one persecutes, Paul the persecutor clearly drew near to the Christian faith and in time became a convert. Interestingly enough, Paul never describes that conversion experience in all of his epistles. It remained for Luke to give it a narrative form, but the Book of Acts was not written until some thirty to thirty-five years after Paul's death. It clearly meets some of Luke's political agenda, so the historical accuracy of Luke's story of Paul's conversion is highly suspect. But the fact of his conversion comes from the pen of Paul himself (Gal. 1:17). That conversion meant that the persecutor sought to be received by those he had previously victimized. It was for Paul not an easy entry into this new faith community.

Paul seemed to be sensitive to this and so did not force himself at once upon the Christians in Jerusalem. Instead he felt a distinct call to be the apostle to the Gentiles. He went first to Arabia, where he stayed three years (Gal. 1:17), perhaps engaged in missionary activity but at least processing the new content of his life before returning to Damascus. Then, according to his own account, he went up to Jerusalem to confer for fifteen days with Peter, the apostle, and James, the Lord's brother (Gal. 1:18–19). After that, he informs us, he stayed in the region of Syria and Cilicia for fourteen years (Gal. 2:1). Those years also appear to have been spent in missionary service, probably as Barnabas's assistant. The second journey to Jerusalem was to deal with the issue of how Gentiles were to be incorporated into the predominantly Jewish Christian community. Paul went to Jerusalem this time, accompanied by his mentor Barnabas and his only Greek assistant, Titus (Gal. 2:1). In Paul's mind a solution was worked out at this meeting. It meant generally that Barnabas and Paul were to go to the Gentiles, while James, Cephas and John were to lead the mission to the Jews. The Jews were not to be freed from the demands of the law. The Gentiles were not to be bound to the demands of the law. It was a tolerable solution for Paul (Gal. 2:2–10).

Returning to his missionary activities, he appears to have split his next two years between Philippi and Thessalonica as an official representative of the Antioch church. But Judaizers from Jerusalem, in violation of the Jerusalem agreement as Paul understood it, continued to press Paul's congregations to adhere to various elements of the law. The sponsoring church in Antioch and even Barnabas himself appear not to have supported Paul as strongly as he wished on this issue. So Paul felt his gospel being compromised by the encroaching demands of a new legalism. Antioch, his home base, seemed to him to be sinking back into being a Jewish church. That was intolerable for Paul, and so he launched into a more Gentile-oriented western missionary tour. His primary tie with the east from that day forward consisted of his commitment to collect an offering for the support of the Jerusalem church. But his orbit of missionary work kept stretching further and further west.

Paul developed a unique missionary style once he was on his own. He would set up a central office in a region and from that center he would develop a process by which he would visit, establish, build and encourage the churches of that region with regularity. Corinth, Ephesus and Rome were his three primary centers or headquarters during the course of his career. Like every church leader he had different problems with different churches. The church in Corinth probably tested him the most with its internal disorders. Philippi probably was the church toward which he felt the most affection. During his active life Paul worked with a number of close associates. Their ranks did not change significantly. Timothy appears to have been his primary assistant, but he also mentions with frequency Titus, Apollo, Silvanus and a couple named Prisca and Aquila, who were probably more important to Paul's missionary success than anyone has yet imagined. This couple appears to have constituted Paul's advance team, moving in and setting up headquarters in all three of Paul's centers of activity in anticipation of his arrival (Rom. 16:3, 1 Cor. 16:19, 2 Tim. 4:19).[13]

Paul fought vigorously to keep his churches free from being dragged back into the legalism of Judaism, which was, in his mind, a compromise of the gospel's integrity. This seems to have been a regular part of his battle in seeking to establish Gentile churches. His letters are filled with vigorous defenses of his apostleship, of his understanding of the gospel and of the Gentile mission of the church. The Book of Acts records three primary missionary journeys that Paul took, but there is a considerable distinction between the chronicle found in the Book of Acts and the one we discern from reading Paul's own words. Christian scholarship almost always sides with Paul when there is a conflict with the Book of Acts. Paul is, after all, writing a first-person account. The Book of Acts is a well-after-the-fact narrative. In any event, the final journey of Paul's life appears to have been under arrest (and perhaps in chains) to the city of Rome in the early sixties. He lived there under house arrest, and the evidence suggests that he died there as a Christian martyr.

Paul, in his letters, left a legacy for the future of Christianity the value of which cannot be overestimated. Recall that when Paul died, no Gospel had yet been written. So Paul is the primary witness to the nature of primitive Christianity. His epistles were formal documents, written to be read in the assembly of the faithful as teaching instruments. His authentic letters are 1 and 2 Thessalonians, though many scholars now identify 1 Thessalonians 2:13–4:2 as his first letter to that church. First Thessalonians 1:1–2:12, 4:3–5:28 thus becomes his second letter and what we call 2 Thessalonians is now seen as his third letter to this same community. All of the Thessalonian letters are generally dated between 50 and 52 and represent the earliest of Paul's surviving work.

Galatians is also an early Pauline letter and should be dated around 53. It expresses the pain that Paul felt when the Judaizers challenged him and threatened to undercut his work. Paul, having seen Antioch sink back into being a Jewish church, was determined to fight vigorously to protect his version of the gospel and the churches for which he was responsible. The Epistle to the Galatians is Paul at his pugilistic best. Here he writes the words "I opposed him [Peter] to his face, because he stood condemned" (Gal. 2:11). Once again, that is hardly "the word of the Lord."

First and second Corinthians are also authentic Pauline works, though few scholars think that what we now have in 1 and 2 Corinthians is the form in which those letters were originally written. Scholars find at least four letters to the church in Corinth buried in the present Corinthian corpus. Some believe they can identify as many as nine. The Corinthian correspondence is generally dated in the mid-fifties. One section of it found in 2 Corinthians 10–13 reveals a Paul so angry that his rigid control has dissolved into rage. Parts of it read as a diatribe.

Romans is the only letter Paul wrote to a church he had neither founded nor visited. He did hope, however, to visit Rome, and so he wrote this epistle to spell out his understanding of the gospel as he proclaimed it. The Epistle to the Romans followed a similar argument to the one that first appeared in the Epistle to the Galatians. It is however more formal, reasoned and magnificent. So complete and passionate is this piece of literature that many refer to this Epistle as "The Gospel according to Paul." In chapters 1–8 it contains Paul's basic understanding of the function of the Christ. In chapters 9–11 Paul discusses the place of the Jews in the drama of salvation. Finally, in chapters 12–15 Paul draws the ethical implications that are present in his gospel. Chapter 16 is a conclusion, but its placement in this Epistle is widely disputed today and many scholars do not think it was an original part of Romans.

The Epistle to Philemon is a tender letter commending a runaway slave, Onesimus, to his former master and is revelatory on many levels. The Epistle to the Philippians is thought by some to be the final authentic Pauline letter. It contains many memorable passages and at least one section that appears to reflect an early Christian hymn (Phil. 2:5–11). This passage reveals some fascinating aspects in the early development of Christology. On one side it introduces hints of divine preexistence for Jesus and on the other, it moves directly from crucifixion to exaltation, with no mention of resurrection whatsoever. It thus reflects what many people believe was a stage in the development of the resurrection traditions in Christianity before things like empty tombs and physical apparitions entered the resurrection story.

It is seriously debated as to whether or not the Epistle to the Colossians is Pauline. So far as I can tell, that debate is an evenly divided one. But in this disputed epistle, the dimensions of the cosmic Christ begin to appear in the material. The Epistle to the Ephesians will develop those ideas more fully. The scholarly world, however, has arrived at a much larger consensus against Ephesians being a Pauline work though there are still one or two holdouts. Finally, no one thinks Hebrews is Pauline despite the fact that the King James Bible once proclaimed it "The Epistle of Paul to the Hebrews." Its style and vocabulary, however, mark it as certainly non-Pauline. In fact, Hebrews is not even an epistle in the sense that it appears not to have been a letter written to anyone. It is much more like a sermon delivered orally in a community and only later written down.

The pastoral Epistles of 1 and 2 Timothy and Titus are also generally not believed to be Pauline. They reveal a structure and an organization in church life that did not exist until well past Paul's day. Despite that, there still are a tiny few who want to make a case for the authenticity of 2 Timothy.[14] The consensus of the New Testament world, however, does not support that conclusion.

When one tries to pull together Paul's major teachings, as revealed in his own writing, one begins with a sense that in Paul's mind sin was an external power or force that separated human life from God. Sin, he believed, entered human life through Adam and enslaved the whole world. It constituted a massive disorientation of God's purpose. The only possible authentic response for Paul to this status of sin was the power of God's grace, which was fully revealed in the self-sacrifice of Christ. The law of the Jews, God's Torah, could never have anticipated this gift of God. So it was the work of the Christ, almost inevitably, to relativize the dogmatic claims of the law upon the consciousness of the Jewish people.

In Paul's mind the Christ was what Adam was meant to be; namely, the authentic human being. Indeed, total self-sacrificing love as revealed in the Christ was for Paul a portrait of authentic humanity. Paul saw this love revealed in the Christ who did not please himself but suffered on behalf of human beings, dying even for the godless. But Paul asserted God had raised this Jesus into the very meaning of God from whence he would remain, available to us forever. His love was and is so total that nothing could separate any of us from the love of God that was in Christ Jesus (Rom. 8:38–39). It was for this reason that God has exalted Jesus to heaven and "bestowed on him the name which is above every name, that at the name of Jesus, every knee shall bow" (Phil. 2:5–11). Those who, in Paul's phrase, are "in Christ" are thus called to model that grace-filled life by living with a self-sacrificing love. This was his understanding of the essence of the Grace of God, which was for Paul God's greatest gift to the world, far surpassing the gift of the law.

For this gospel and in the service of this Lord, Paul was quite content to give his life, his energy and his devotion. He willingly endured incredible abuse, beatings, shipwrecks, danger from robbers on land and storms at sea, and finally, death (2 Cor. 11:24–29). For Paul was convinced that "to live is Christ and to die is gain" (Phil. 1:21). His was a tremendous witness. He stands next to Jesus himself, as the architect of the Christianity that most of us have experienced.

That is a brief description of the external Paul. But what did this Christian revelation look like internally to him? That is a rather different story. Though no one will ever know for sure, Paul has certainly left us hints and so we turn to these to try to reconstruct the inner man. What follows is speculative, but it is speculation that is not without foundation. I think we have to try to recreate the inner person in Paul if we are to throw light on the way he understood both himself and the Christ figure. We need to penetrate the mystery of Paul's zeal, his persecution of the

Christians and his violent conversion. Each of these is an obvious element in his personality that has remained unexamined at least in a radical way for far too long. Because of Paul's religious importance, the divine inspiration attributed to his words and the need the Church has had to build its creeds and doctrines on his letters, the humanity of Paul has remained hidden in the shadows, covered by layers of piety, fear and repression. It is my conviction that this humanity provides the clue to understanding everything he did and everything he wrote, and it is thus imperative that the inner Paul be discussed openly. So into the psyche of Paul I now seek to go, led to the degree that it is possible by his own words, building on an inference here and a hint there. I base this analysis primarily on my conviction that basic personalities do not change dramatically in the course of a lifetime. The content, convictions and attitudes of life may shift, but they express themselves through the same basic personality structure. We know much about the converted Christian Paul and because we do, we can thus know far more than many have imagined about the pre-Christian Paul.

I see the young Paul as a religious zealot. That is easy to document because he acknowledges it himself (Gal. 1:11–14). One does not erupt in persecuting fury in adulthood unless zealotry has been part of one's nature for a long time. He describes himself as zealous for the law, as eager to move beyond all of his peers in devotion to his studies (Gal. 1:14). I suspect that when he went to Jerusalem he, as a diaspora Jew, had to defend his orthodox convictions against those whose vision of religious purity assumed that for anyone to have lived outside Judea was to have compromised the integrity of Jewish practice. This defensiveness, found in the assertion that he was a "Hebrew of the Hebrews" (Phil. 3:5), was a familiar defense employed by

Jews of the exile to demonstrate that their faith had not been corrupted by alien practices. Yet, in his childhood as a resident of Tarsus, where his religion was not indigenous, to maintain his deeply felt Jewish convictions took courage and zeal. It also helped to enforce the defensive conviction that he was in touch with a truth that, at least in his mind, had relativized all other versions of truth. That is, I submit, the very stuff that creates the fanatic. That is also the behavior of one whose personal being has been submerged inside an imposed interpretive framework. That framework serves two purposes: it prevents ones insecurity from being compromised, and it allows the hidden person to remain hidden and not to have to endure the uniqueness of his or her own being. Fanatics are almost always institutionally identified persons. Their personal being has been subsumed inside their identification with that tradition with which they have surrounded themselves.

Religious fanaticism, properly understood, is a means and a method of survival. It is a public proclamation that the person you are is so insignificant, or that the person you know yourself to be is so unacceptable, that you have hidden from your fears inside the protective armor of a religious frame of reference. Every religious system produces some adherents who are this way. They are the ones who cannot step out of the role that they have used to define themselves. They are almost robotlike in their religious adherence. They cannot tolerate those who might question the truth or the authenticity of what they have defined themselves to be. Paul, as a young man studying in his synagogue school, must have manifested these characteristics. When he moved to Jerusalem, the city where religious devotion was almost normative, these tendencies probably were accelerated. Paul took second place to no one in piety, devotion and zeal. Yet, the religious practices he adopted were more and more those of rigid control. One has to wonder what it was that made obedience to and control by the external authority of the law so essential to the survival of this man.

Perhaps we have a clue to this mystery in Paul's reference to the fact that he possessed "a thorn in the flesh" that he called "a messenger of Satan" (2 Cor. 12:7). Perhaps it is also echoed in his persistent negativity toward his body and his flesh. "O wretched man that I am, who shall deliver me from this body of death" (Rom. 7:24). In other places Paul talks about the need for the sinful body to be destroyed so that we might no longer be enslaved to sin (Rom. 6:6). He urged his readers not to let sin "reign in your mortal bodies to make you obey their passions" (Rom. 6:12). He spoke of the need to "pummel my body and subdue it" (1 Cor. 9:27). He talked of his desire to be cleansed "from every defilement of body" (2 Cor. 7:1). Paul's concept of sin as an alien power that has control over his life also appears to be related to his own self-understanding. Sin, he believed, could be controlled only by the law. His was a religion of suppression. Something unacceptable within himself had to be contained. That is the prescription for a zealotry that produces religious rigidity—for there to be a threat to that control system is the primary requirement that will turn such a one into a zealous persecutor. Each of these elements is in Paul. If there is to be a resolution other than constant warfare to this kind of powerful internal tension, it would normally come only through a cataclysmic reorientation and reevaluation that would be seen as a powerful conversion experience. Persecution or reorientation are the only alternatives for such a personality. This, we are all aware, also appears to be a part of the history of Paul. He has all of the elements that produce the certifiable religious fanatic. His life is marked by a strong adherence to a rigid religion of control: the zeal necessary to keep things under lock and key and the violence that comes with any threat that challenges this system are clearly identified parts of his personality. The mentality of the persecutor is born in this psychological makeup. It fits Paul of Tarsus to a T. It also begs the question of what the reality was that drove Paul internally and thus created this pivotal figure in Christian history.

The suggestions throughout history have abounded. While there has been little agreement on a specific cause, it is fair to say that the weight of scholarship seeking answers has fastened on either some type of physical ailment or on some kind of psychological problem. The physical suggestions have included epilepsy, poor eyesight, a chronic eye infection, recurring fevers or a speech impediment. Yet none of these proposed explanations seems to be convincing when one considers the physical rigor of Paul's life. He walked to most of the cities on his journeys, sometimes being on the roads for weeks or months at a time. He slept on roadsides or in inns and ate whatever food he could find. It is difficult to conceive of Paul having a serious physical malady that would haunt him as he indicates his "thorn in the flesh" haunted him and still do the physical things that we know he did.

When we move from physical explanations to psychological explanations, a richer and more fanciful set of possibilities emerges. The suggestions here have ranged from those who think it resulted from mild despair over the refusal of the Jews to respond to his gospel all the way to a form of depression or mental illness that would have been interpreted in his day as the presence of a very real and quite external demon. Yet here again we find no evidence in either his life or his writing that he suffered from any immobilizing psychological dysfunction. He organized his life in a purposeful way, carried out his responsibilities in a timely fashion, advocated his cause and defended his point of view appropriately.

Jerome Murphy-O'Connor, a Roman Catholic Pauline scholar, admits this. But in O'Connor's mind that leaves him with the task of identifying Paul's "thorn in the flesh" and the reason for his self-negativity as "the opposition to his ministry." This, he incredulously asserts, becomes the "only hypothesis for which a serious case can be made."[15] That is a woefully inadequate solution. Such an explanation in no way accounts for Paul's preconversion fanaticism, his violent persecutions of those who threatened his religious control system or his powerful conversion experience. It assumes that the negativity he expressed toward himself did not appear until after his missionary efforts began to be thwarted. It is a suggestion so naive, it prompts suspicion that it, too, is a part of some suppressive system of control.

There is only one theory that accounts for the evidence and that is that there was something that Paul experienced in his being itself, which he deemed to be dark, evil, unacceptable, imposed upon him from outside himself, unresponsive to his own efforts to cast it off and therefore requiring a rigid control lest it overwhelm him. This reality also had to be something that did not lower Paul's energy level or his physical competence. It had to be something not readily visible to others. It was something he wrestled with internally, but not necessarily externally. Yet it must have defined his very nature to himself. If that is so, then it would be quite impossible for it not to be revealed in his writings, and we should find hints of it all through the Pauline corpus. I think we do. I can only speculate about its origins, but Paul's writings do document its reality. Of all the options that might account for this reality and that would satisfy the prerequisites, only one seems to me to fit every detail. So I invite my readers to consider the possibility that Paul was a homosexual man who believed that this was an affliction imposed upon him that had to be repressed if it could not be changed. The only way I know to test this supposition is by assuming its truth and then seeing if it fits the data.[16]

If Paul was a gay man, then when he was a young teenager he, like thousands before and after him, would begin to be aware that he was different and, in his mind, not normal, as normalcy was defined in his world. It would probably start in the recognition that he felt himself not to fit the mold of the majority. His desires, when he allowed them to surface, were not what he had been taught were acceptable. Those desires also frightened him. He did not know how to talk about his feelings or whether he should talk about them at all, and if so, with whom. He surely had heard his parents' comments on those whom they regarded as afflicted with Paul's "malady" enough times to know that, far from being accepting, they would be horrified. The common wisdom of his day condemned homosexuality as abnormal, sick or depraved. It was made the butt of cruel jokes and demeaning laughter. Paul knew that his synagogue leaders would also find the subject anathema, for that is the way they had talked about it in the classes on the Torah. The Torah condemned in no uncertain terms the possibility that a man might like to "lie with a man as with a woman." That was "an abomination" (Lev. 18:22). Those who did these things were "defiled" (Lev. 18:24). When God punished the nation for these sins, the land "vomited out" these inhabitants (Lev. 18:25). The Torah went on to pronounce both of the partners in such a liaison to be worthy of death (Lev. 20:13). This was for Paul the final word to be spoken on this subject. The word of the Lord in the Torah was clear. There was no debate beyond that point.

Paul, I suspect, was horrified by his feelings. I find no reason to think that he had experience doing what he clearly believed was a dreadful thing, but those desires had to be repressed since they would not go away. So Paul, by the might of concentration, kept these feelings at bay by day, only to discover that they emerged in his dreams at night. Adolescent dreams, especially wet dreams, can be disturbing even to those whose fantasies are judged to be normal. They can be terrifying when accompanied by fantasies that are thought to be abnormal. They were explained by suggesting that some demonic power from outside had taken hold of that life and forced upon it a desire that he knew was wrong. Echoes of this explanation as we have noted can be heard in Paul time after time.

Today we know that homosexual desire is the reality of at least some five to ten percent of the population at all times and in all places throughout human history. But that knowledge was not available to Paul. I suspect he felt that he was the only one who had ever been afflicted by such "a messenger of Satan." Like most people who have to wrestle with what they do not understand, I am certain that Paul was scared, even horrified by the realization that he was experiencing desire for something he had been taught to regard as so totally evil. He defended himself by believing that this was not his own desire, but that of some demonic power that possessed him. He would, therefore, do battle against this evil impulse with every resource his religion offered to him. This, I would wager, is what motivated Paul into a passion for the law. I am confident that he had read in the Books of the Maccabees that Joseph was praised because "by mental effort he overcame sexual desire" (4 Macc. 2:2). Later in the same apocryphal work, the author of Maccabees said, "The temperate mind can conquer the drives of the emotions and quench the flames of frenzied desires and, by nobility of reason, spurn all domination by the emotions" (4 Macc. 3:17–18). These works of the Maccabees were very popular in the first century and were favorite reading for serious students of the law. Paul may have counted on their wisdom to help him bank the flames of his unacceptable desire. So negative were these desires to Paul that he saw suppression as his only hope. He had to recognize the fact that according to the law he studied and treasured, he was possessed by an evil one. In that state, the law he honored and whose authority he accepted, judged him as one who was, in fact, not worthy of life. If this power ever gained full possession of his will, he was doomed. So Paul vowed to arm himself with the law as the only way he could contend against this evil power. Perhaps this is why he adopted a frenzied devotion to the traditions of the law and reinforced them by claiming literal truth for every aspect of his faith system. Paul was on his way to being a fanatic. It was only thus that this dark side of his personality could be kept at bay.

This stance won him the recognition of his schoolmasters and synagogue leaders. They approved of and praised him for his devotion. Their response encouraged him into more and more works of supererogation. He thrived under their attention. The more approval he achieved, the more passionately he studied the Torah. He read the commentaries of antiquity. He meditated on the texts of his tradition. I suspect he externalized his control system as so many religious fanatics do by dressing himself in the most conservative attire of the tradition he represented. This forced people everywhere to relate to him as he wished to be defined, a passionately committed religious zealot. I suspect he worshiped at the synagogue regularly and at every opportunity, coming early and leaving late. I am confident that he devoured what his teachers had to say to him. If true to the prototype of the religious fanatic, he developed a sharp tongue that was quick to demolish and to condemn those who might compromise or even shade the law. I suspect he exhibited his deepest loathing, as do most fanatics, not for the infidel, but for those Jews who were lax or liberal about the law. Describing himself in this period Paul wrote, "You have heard no doubt of my earlier life in Judaism. . . . I advanced in Judaism beyond many among my people of the same age, for I was more zealous for the traditions of my ancestors" (Gal. 1:13–14).

I have met religious zealots like this many times in my life. The content of their zealotry varied widely, but the emotional tone was quite similar. They have wrapped themselves tightly in their version of unchallenged truth. Their religious system has provided them with a security shield that enables them to hide something they cannot face. It might be their own dark side. It might be that sense of radical aloneness in a hostile universe that produces hysteria unless some religious coping mechanism is developed. It might mean that they have no confidence in their own being, so that they try to submerge it into the being of their religious system. Whatever the motivation, it is almost always the mark of religious zealots to be enraged when their systems are shaken.

I remember well a young evangelical I met in another English-speaking nation, who seemed to follow me all over the capital city of that country. At almost every lecture he tried to attack my integrity personally by interrupting with hostile comments, and he frantically tried to gain an audience afterward so that he could set my hearers straight. He was in his own development, still defending a literal eye-witness version of the gospels, while passionately resisting the insights of Darwin. He was reminiscent of what the young, rigid Paul must have appeared to be, fragile, scared, with a defensiveness that manifested itself as aggressiveness. It was clear that this evangelical, like Paul, could not stand or tolerate the possibility that I might be right, for that would mean that he must be wrong. If he was wrong, his entire security system would collapse, and he would have to deal with whatever it was that this security system was keeping deeply hidden and deeply suppressed.

That was quite clearly the threat that those Jewish people who responded to Jesus of Nazareth created for Paul. The Jewish Christians relativized the claims of the law. They asserted that grace was the key to one's relationship with God. At the heart of their message was a belief that God loved them just as they were. That presented Paul with a frightening picture of freedom. Christ died for them, the Christians asserted, while they were sinners. God did not require that they perfect themselves according to the words of the Torah. It was a deeply disturbing claim.

Paul was quite sure that God could not love him. He was quite sure that if he were to loosen the bands by which he had bound himself inside the law, then these demonic passions would leap upon him and consume him. So the very presence of these so-called followers of the "way" threatened Paul's security system.[17] At first he tried to ignore them, but they seemed to grow and to thrive, and the freedom that they exhibited posed a violent danger to Paul.

On some level, however, this Christianity must also have been just a little bit attractive. As soon as its appeal was experienced, however, I suspect Paul would slam the door shut on such an idea. Indeed, I would guess that he regarded that attractiveness simply as one more temptation of the devil luring him into a vulnerable place. Finally, the growing power of the Christian movement, together with the highly unacceptable attraction to the freedom about which these Christians talked, combined to cause Paul to identify the Christians as a threat to all he cherished. If they succeeded, Paul would fail. If they were right, Paul was wrong. If they prevailed, Paul would be destroyed.

The hints of why Paul felt this so deeply are all over his epistles. There was a sense in which Paul saw himself as an impostor, as unknown, as dying and as punished (2 Cor. 6:9–10). Those words are the words of one who knows that who he is is unacceptable and thus worthy only of punishment and death. Where else would such feelings come from in the life of one so devoted to living the Torah? Paul said, "I do not understand my own actions. For I do not do what I want, but I do the very thing I hate. . . . But in fact it is no longer I that do it, but sin that dwells within me. For I know that nothing good dwells within me that is in my flesh. I can will what is right, but I cannot do it" (Rom. 7:15ff). Paul comforted himself by articulating the conclusion that since "it is no longer I that do it but sin that dwells within me" (Rom. 7:20), I must be exonerated. I regard these words as deeply revelatory.

Paul goes on to use both a word and a phrase that are equally revealing. This sin, he asserts, dwells in my "members" (Rom. 7:23). The Greek word used here is "melos," which means a bodily part or an appendage of the body. His members, he argues, will not obey his mind. There is only one bodily part or appendage of the body which does not obey the mind, and that is the genitalia. This member is controlled by glands that respond to the hormonal messages from the brain. So Paul urged his followers not to present their members "as instruments of wickedness," and later he says "present your members as slaves to righteousness for sanctification" (Rom. 6:13, 19). Sexual arousal cannot always be controlled, and sexual potency cannot always be achieved by an act of the mind. Paul knew this, but because he had no other categories of explanation and because homosexual fantasies and desires were anathema to him, he saw himself engaged in spiritual warfare against powers and principalities that did not abide by the controls of the Torah. He spoke with both hostility and disgust toward his flesh and its desires. "Consider yourself dead to sin," he wrote to the Romans (6:11). "I am carnal," he said, and "sold under sin" (Rom. 7:14). "Nothing good dwells within me, that is in my flesh," he stated (Rom. 7:18). "Wretched man that I am," he exclaimed, "who will deliver me from this body of death?" (Rom. 7:24). In other places Paul said, "I punish my own body and subdue it" (1 Cor. 9:27). He wrote to the Galatians, urging them not to gratify the desires of the flesh (5:16), and then described the works of the flesh in a long list, but at the top of that list are sexual sins "fornication, impurity and licentiousness" (5:19).

The Christians, to Paul, loosened the control that kept what he described as "these fears within" in check (2 Cor. 7:5). The very existence of the Christians called his control system into question and thus threatened his ability to keep his homosexual demons repressed. Like many deeply controlled and repressed gay people after him, he struck out to persecute and to remove those whose existence threatened to destroy his facade. So he erupted. In his own words, "I violently persecuted the church of God and was trying to destroy it" (Gal. 1:13). No one ever persecutes something that does not both threaten that person deeply and, at the same time, attract that person subtly. If Paul was able to destroy Christianity, his defenses would remain intact. But if Christianity proved to be successful in removing those defenses and enabled the frightened, fearful, trembling, scared person who lived beneath them to be revealed, he would be driven to a violent act, perhaps of suicide. For that kind of self-revelation was judged sufficient to make him unfit even to live any longer. The only alternative to this self-destruction would be conversion and that would be possible only if he could know that his self-revelation did not make him rejectable or unacceptable, or if he learned that nothing in either the heights or in the depths could separate him from the love of God. Given his years of fearful hiding, such a conversion would inevitably come as a traumatic, violent, blinding, reorienting experience.

We have read the Bible for so long without psychologically trained eyes that it seems almost inappropriate to turn that modern lens onto its pages now. But turn it we must. A persecuting personality is revelatory of deep psychological conflict. A violent conversion is revelatory of that conflict coming to an unanticipated resolution.

What does Paul say that gives us a clue to that conversion? He tells us nothing about a Damascus Road experience. He never mentions Ananias, who, Luke suggested, tended him and baptized him. All of these stories are narratives that Luke created some thirty-plus years after Paul's death. Paul had no chance to speak about their authenticity. But what the converted Paul does say is that conversion means that he has joined the converted ones who "belong to Christ" (1 Cor. 3:23). He does say that we "are beside ourselves . . . for God" (2 Cor. 5:13). He does insist that "Christ died for all" so that all might live "for him" (2 Cor. 5:15). He does insist that our old self was crucified with him and united with him in a resurrection (Rom. 6:5–6). He does consider himself dead to sin, but alive to God (Rom. 6:11). He does assert that sin no longer dwells in his body to make him obey its passions (Rom. 6:12). He does proclaim that once his "members" were slaves to impurity, but now they are slaves to righteousness (Rom. 6:19). He does say that "Christ Jesus has made me his own" (Phil. 3:12). He does say that "nothing can separate him from the love of God" (Rom. 8:39) and that "the love of God controls him" (2 Cor. 5:14), and he does assert that "no one who believes in Him (Christ) shall be put to shame" (Rom. 10:11).

What was the content of Paul's conversion? Since Paul does not relate that experience directly, we are again left to speculate. Was he speaking of his own conversion when he wrote, "I know a person who fourteen years ago was caught up to the third heaven whether in the body or out of the body I do not know, God knows" (2 Cor. 12:2), or when he suggested that when one turns to God "the veil is removed" (2 Cor. 3:16)? Was he alluding to his conversion when he said that God has "shone in our hearts to give the light of the knowledge of the glory of Christ in the face of Jesus Christ" (2 Cor. 4:6)? Paul believed that he had been given the grace of Christ. It was not his doing. It was God's gracious act. It convinced him that there was no condemnation, not only for him but for all "who are in Christ Jesus" (Rom. 8:1). In a very revealing way he asserted that even his "nakedness," which I interpret to mean that even the secrets of his body if fully revealed, could never separate him from the love of God. In that he pronounced himself more than a conqueror "through him who loved us" (Rom. 8:35–37).

Luke later, I suspect, took these hints from Paul and created the drama of the Damascus Road experience. It was, I believe, psychologically, if not literally, accurate. He portrayed Paul as "ravaging the church by entering house after house; dragging off both men and women" to prison (Acts 8:3). He described him later as "breathing threats and murder against the disciples of the Lord" (Acts 9:1). Then conversion came, "A light from heaven flashed around him. He fell to the ground and heard a voice" (Acts 9:3–4). The voice was identified as "Jesus, whom you are persecuting" (Acts 9:5). Those traveling with him saw nothing (Acts

9:7). Paul also could see nothing, as he was blinded, and so he was led by the hand to Damascus. For three days he lived in that darkness, neither eating nor drinking (Acts 9:8–9). His resurrection was to be reminiscent, at least in time, of the resurrection of his Lord, who also lived in darkness, the darkness of death, for three days.

Next, by way of an introductory vision, he received word that Ananias would come to restore his sight. When Ananias arrived, Luke said that scales seemed to fall from Paul's eyes. He was then baptized and was filled with the Holy Spirit (Acts 9:10–19).

That was Luke's version of what occurred in Paul when his enormous inner conflict was finally resolved. Paul discovered that his fears, his dark side, his unacceptable desires were now known, accepted, loved and transformed. He had been invited into God's love, "just as I am, without one plea."[18] The love of God made known in Christ had embraced him. The inner turmoil was resolved. Paul was set free, not from his essential nature, but from the judgment, the self-loathing, the rejection, the death that he assumed was his deserving. He was now free to live, free to love and free to be, because "Christ has made me his own" (Phil. 3:12).

The passage of Paul that drives me so powerfully to this conclusion is found in that part of the Pauline corpus that modern literalists, seeking to justify their fear and rejection of homosexual persons, quote as one of the scriptural justifications for their continuing prejudice. These are the deeply revealing verses found in the opening lines of Paul's epistle to the Romans (1:18–32). After arguing that the righteous live by faith, Paul develops a strange line of reasoning designed to show that God has revealed himself to all people through the creation. Then he goes on to say that those who do not discern the truth of God through creation and thus do not worship God properly are, as their punishment, given over to lust, iniquity and the misuse of their bodies among themselves (Rom. 1:24). "Therefore," Paul continued, "God gave them up to degrading passions. Their women exchanged natural intercourse for unnatural and in the same way also the men, giving up natural intercourse with women, were consumed with passion for one another. Men committed shameless acts with men and received in their own persons the due penalty for their error" (Rom. 1:26–27).

Paul, we noted earlier, had never been to Rome. Perhaps he had heard from other travelers that homosexuality was widely practiced in the city, as in so many urban areas of the world, so he interpreted that in the light of his own knowledge and experience. It was God's judgment on those who did not discern God correctly. That negativity is, I suspect, what had fueled his own passionate attempt to master the Torah, to advance beyond his fellows in the zeal for the traditions of his ancestors. That is why he was a fanatic for his understanding of truth and why he was driven to make sure that he worshiped properly. Judgment, he argued, would be apart from the law for those who did not know the law, and it would be under the law for those who did. But this judgment was designed to convince all that apart from the infinite love of God and the grace of Christ, there was no hope. These verses are, I believe, indicative of Paul's inner struggle, which led him finally to assert, "Wretched man that I am, who will rescue me from this body of death? Thanks be to God through Jesus Christ our Lord" (Rom. 7:24–25). Paul wrote these words to the Romans on the other side of the victory that had been won. But he also wrote them conscious of the struggle he had endured and in terms of his very limited understanding of the reality that defined him to himself.

The only thing that makes sense out of Paul's fanatical life as a Torah-observing Jew, his time as a persecutor, his violent conversion and the ecstasy of his understanding of what it means to live his life "in Christ," is that Paul was possessed by what he believed was an inner demon. I do not believe it could have been epilepsy or any other physical handicap. I see nothing in his writings that reveals mental illness, manic depression or paranoia. I do not believe he could have endured the rigors of his life if he had had some debilitating physical or mental trauma. To locate Paul's "thorn in the flesh" as the opposition of the Jews or the failure of the Judaizers to respond to his proclamation of the gospel does not take into consideration the same psychological forces that are manifested in his zeal, his acts of persecution or his conversion.

Only one thing seems to me to fit the known data. Paul lived in the grip of an internal identity crisis that would not be visible to the naked eye and that would not affect his physical well-being. It had to be a malady that would be defined and addressed in the way that first-century Jewish people would have defined it and addressed it. It had to account for the self-rejection and self-deprecating aspects of Paul's writing. It had to produce that frantic attempt at suppression with the use of layers of piety, prayers and study. It had to be so deeply a part of Paul's being that it could not be either "shed" or "cured." It had to find expression in what he said and did, for it was part of his very being. It had to be resolved, not by being changed, but by being accepted. Nothing else fits the data in my mind nearly so well as the possibility, I would say probability, that Paul was a gay man. He was a gay man who had been taught by the Torah to hate homosexual people, who believed that being homosexual was a distortion of the image of God within him and that it resulted from improper worship. Nothing else accounts for the Paul who vowed to overcome this "messenger of Satan," who argued that this reality that he experienced within his very being was not himself but "sin" that dwelled in him, and who became first a religious zealot and fanatic and then, when a Christian movement began to destabilize his rigorous security system, a persecutor of these Christians. Nothing else makes sense of a conversion experience so total that Paul never wanted the law again to corrupt the freedom that he had found in Christ Jesus. Nothing else comes close to explaining how deeply he felt about those Christians who wanted to drift back into being legalistic, law-abiding observers of the Torah, who compromised the gospel to keep unity inside the churches by acceding to the demands of the Judaizers from Jerusalem.

It was, I believe, a repressed gay man named Paul of Tarsus who had been taught by his religion and his society to hate what he knew he was, who ultimately gave to the Christian faith its concept of grace, as the undeserved, unmerited love of God found in Christ Jesus. It was one who was confident that if people knew him as he really was, rejection would be his ultimate destiny, who feared that this Jesus could not possibly accept him. Yet the God of love had grasped him, embraced him, called him to be that which God had created him to be. That was the message of converting, life-changing power that Paul heard. That was also his understanding of grace, the pure grace of God.

The message of grace is a powerful and universal message. We need to recognize, if this speculative reconstruction of Paul is accurate, that while only some five to ten percent of the population might be homosexual, almost everyone living has a dark side—a *shadow side* as Carl Jung would call it, that they feel, if it were to be known, would make them unacceptable. Most people hide from themselves and from others based on some assessment of their own deep-seated sense of self-rejection. That is a human and universal experience. The God that Paul believed he met in Jesus Christ invites not just self-rejecting gay people, but all people to come as you are, to live inside the infinite love of God, to accept your shadows as part of who you are and to live as one who is accepted, loved and transformed. That was the gift articulated as the essence of Christ by Saul/Paul of Tarsus. It was indeed a mighty gift that still brings good news to the world. This gift can be found in Paul's words. It is to the reading of these words which this volume commends you. But those words must be read in the context of the complexities that marked the life of the one who authored them. By introducing you briefly to Paul, both externally and internally, my hope has been that you will read his words with a deeper understanding.

NOTES

1. Dio Cassius, *Roman History*. Translated by E. Cary. (Loeb Classical Library, Cambridge: Harvard, 1924, 1925).

2. Appian History 5.7. Translated by H. White. (LCL, Cambridge: Harvard, 1913).

3. Pliny (Book 5, 92) calls Tarsus "a free city." Translated by H. Rackhan. (LCL, Cambridge: Harvard, 1944–52).

4. Dio Chrysostom Discourses NH 34.8. Translated by J. W. Cohoon and H. L. Crosby. (LCL, Cambridge: Harvard, 1949–51).

5. M. Hengel and R. Deines, *The Pre-Christian Paul* (London: SCM Press, 1991).

6. T. Callander, The Tarsian Orations of Dio Chrysostom, Journal of Hellenic Studies, vol. 24: 64, 65.

7. *The Interpreter's Dictionary of the Bible,* vol. 4, (New York: Abingdon Press, 1962), 518. Article by M. J. Mellink.

8. Jerome Murphy-O'Connor, *Paul, A Critical Life,* (Oxford: Clarendon Press), 42. See also T. J. Leary, "Paul's Improper Name," *New Testament Studies* 38, 467–69.

9. In Philippians 4:3 Paul addresses one whom he identifies as "true yokefellow." The Greek word for *yokefellow* may be understood as a proper name, Syzygus. In Philemon 1:11 Paul plays on the name Onesimus, which also means "useful."

10. E. Hennecke and W. Schneemelcher, *New Testament Apocrypha* (London: Lutterworth, 1965).

11. J. Murphy-O'Connor, *Paul, A Critical Life*, 47.

12. S. K. Stowers, *Letter Writing in Greco-Roman Antiquity* (Philadelphia: Westminster, 1986).

13. J. Murphy-O'Connor, *Paul, A Critical Life*, 234. Please note that in earlier revisions of the Bible Prisca was rendered Priscilla.

14. J. Murphy-O'Connor seeks to make this case. See pp. 357–58. I was unconvinced by his argument.

15. J. Murphy-O'Connor, *Paul, A Critical Life*, 321–22.

16. I first offered this possibility in 1991 in a book entitled *Rescuing the Bible from Fundamentalism* (San Francisco: Harper-Collins). The response was predictable, and it ranged from ridicule to incredible hostility. I have in the years since that book's publication had the opportunity to consider the negative statements of my critics and to redefine my original ideas. I will do that in this essay. I remain convinced that this is the clue that unlocks the meaning of Paul.

17. In the Book of Acts Christians were referred to as those who followed "The Way." See Acts 9:2, 19:9–23, 24:22.

18. Words from a familiar evangelical hymn.

BIBLIOGRAPHY

Barrett, C. K. *The New Testament Background: Selected Documents.* London: SPCK, 1987.

Conzelmann, H. *I Corinthians—A Commentary on the First Epistle to the Corinthians.* Philadelphia: Fortress Press, 1975.

Cullman, O. *Peter: Disciple, Apostle, Martyr.* London: SCM, 1953.

Dodd, C. H. *The Epistle of Paul to the Romans.* London: Hodder and Stoughton, 1949.

Ellis, E. E. *Paul's Use of the Old Testament.* Grand Rapids, MI: Eerdsmams, 1981.

Furnish, V. P. *II Corinthians,* Anchor Bible. Garden City, NY: Doubleday, 1984.

Haenchen, Ernst. *The Acts of the Apostles.* Philadelphia: Westminster, 1971.

Hennecke, E., and Scneemelcher, W. *New Testament Apocrypha.* London: Lutterworth, 1965.

Knox, J. *Chapters in a Life of Paul.* Nashville: Abingdon, 1950.

Kummel, W. G. *Introduction to the New Testament.* London: SCM, 1975.

BIBLIOGRAPHY

Meeks, W. *The First Urban Christians: The Social World of the Apostle Paul*. New Haven, CT: Yale University Press, 1983.

Murphy-O'Connor, Jerome. *Paul, A Critical Life*. Oxford: Clarendon Press, 1996.

Nock, A. D. *St. Paul*. New York: Harper & Bros., 1937.

Perrin, N. *Rediscovering the Teaching of Jesus*. New York: Harper & Row, 1976.

Phillips, J. B. *Letters to Young Churches*. London, Fontana, 1955.

Sandmel, S. *The Genius of Paul*. New York: Farrar, Straus & Cudahy, 1958.

Sherwin-White, A. N. *Roman Society and Roman Law in the New Testament*. Oxford: Clarendon Press, 1963.

Spong, J. S. *Rescuing the Bible from Fundamentalism*. San Francisco: HarperCollins, 1991.

Stendahl, K. *Paul Among Jews and Gentiles*. Philadelphia: Fortress, 1977.

A NOTE ABOUT THE BIBLICAL
TEXTS

In this volume we have tried to place the work of Paul into
a historical context so that our readers may experience the
ways in which his thought grew over the time of his ministry. That is, however, not a simple assignment. There is
great debate in academic circles over how many separate
letters have been incorporated into what we now call First
and Second Corinthians, Philippians, and even First and
Second Thessalonians. There is debate as to whether the
sixteenth chapter of Romans was actually a part of Paul's
original letter to the Church in Rome. There is debate over
whether any part of either Colossians or Ephesians is actually Pauline. The scholarly debate on the Pauline authorship
of Colossians is evenly divided, while a majority of scholars
today do not acknowledge the Pauline authorship of Ephesians. There is an almost universal consensus that Paul is
not the author of what we call the Pastoral Epistles, First
and Second Timothy and Titus. No scholar I know of today
would still contend that the Epistle to the Hebrews is from
the hand of Paul. However, because the Riverhead Sacred

Text series uses the King James version of the New Testament, in which all of these works were considered to be written by Paul, we have included them in this volume—though not in the order found in the King James Bible.

The authority for our order is basically adapted from the work of Dr. James Veitch, professor of Religious Studies at Victoria University in Wellington, New Zealand. Parts of Dr. Veitch's order would also not be unanimously saluted. Most New Testament scholars suggest that in our present biblical texts there are at least four, or parts of four, separate letters in our two Epistles to the Corinthians. Dr. Veitch's study has led him to conclusions that are much more complicated. He proposes seven separate letters and places them in the chronological order listed below. The reader might experiment by reading the Corinthian Epistles in Dr. Veitch's proposed order to discern how the thought of Paul developed.

1. 2 Cor. 6:14–7:1
2. 1 Cor. 1–16
3. 2 Cor. 2:14–6:13, 7:2–4
4. 2 Cor. 10–13
5. 2 Cor. 1:1–2:13, 7:5–16
6. 2 Cor. 8
7. 2 Cor. 9

Dr. Veitch also suggests that three separate letters are identifiable in what we call the Epistle to the Philippians, and these were eventually blended into a single Epistle by later reductors. It might be helpful in exploring this possibility to read them in the order he proposes on the following page for new insights.

1. Phil. 3:2–4:9
2. Phil. 4:10–20
3. Phil. 1:1–3:1

All of these ideas are roundly debated. We list them not to endorse them but to make our readers aware of the debate and of the new possibilities that are offered here.

It is our hope that in calling the attention of our readers to the dimensions of this New Testament debate and by proposing a rough but not universally agreed to chronology, we can capture a sense of the man Paul as he struggled to express his faith and his understanding of Jesus at different points in his life's pilgrimage.

1 THESSALONIANS

CHAPTER ONE

Paul, and Sĭl-vā'nŭs, and Tĭ-mō'thē ŭs, unto the church of the Thĕs'-så-lō'nĭ-ăns *which is* in God the Father, and *in* the Lord Jesus Christ: Grace *be* unto you, and peace, from God our Father, and the Lord Jesus Christ.

2. We give thanks to God always for you all, making mention of you in our prayers;

3. Remembering without ceasing your work of faith, and labor of love, and patience of hope in our Lord Jesus Christ, in the sight of God and our Father;

4. Knowing, brethren beloved, your election of God.

5. For our gospel came not unto you in word only, but also in power, and in the Holy Ghost, and in much assurance; as ye know what manner of men we were among you for your sake.

6. And ye became followers of us, and of the Lord, having received the word in much affliction, with joy of the Holy Ghost:

7. So that ye were ensamples to all that believe in Macedonia and Á-ɛhā'i̯á.

8. For from you sounded out the word of the Lord not only in Macedonia and Á-ɛhā'i̯á, but also in every place your faith to God-ward is spread abroad; so that we need not to speak any thing.

9. For they themselves show of us what manner of entering in we had unto you, and how ye turned to God from idols to serve the living and true God;

10. And to wait for his Son from heaven, whom he raised from the dead, *even* Jesus, which delivered us from the wrath to come.

CHAPTER TWO

For yourselves, brethren, know our entrance in unto you, that it was not in vain:

2. But even after that we had suffered before, and were shamefully entreated, as ye know, at Phĭ-lĭp'pī, we were bold in our God to speak unto you the gospel of God with much contention.

3. For our exhortation *was* not of deceit, nor of uncleanness, nor in guile:

4. But as we were allowed of God to be put in trust with the gospel, even so we speak; not as pleasing men, but God, which trieth our hearts.

5. For neither at any time used we flattering words, as ye know, nor a cloak of covetousness; God *is* witness:

6. Nor of men sought we glory, neither of you, nor *yet* of others, when we might have been burdensome, as the apostles of Christ.

7. But we were gentle among you, even as a nurse cherisheth her children:

8. So being affectionately desirous of you, we were willing to have imparted unto you, not the gospel of God only, but also our own souls, because ye were dear unto us.

9. For ye remember, brethren, our labor and travail: for laboring night and day, because we would not be chargeable unto any of you, we preached unto you the gospel of God.

10. Ye *are* witnesses, and God *also*, how holily and justly and unblamably we behaved ourselves among you that believe:

11. As ye know how we exhorted and comforted and charged every one of you, as a father *doth* his children,

12. That ye would walk worthy of God, who hath called you unto his kingdom and glory.

13. For this cause also thank we God without ceasing, because, when ye received the word of God which ye heard of us, ye received *it* not *as* the word of men, but, as it is in truth, the word of God, which effectually worketh also in you that believe.

14. For ye, brethren, became followers of the churches of God which in Judea are in Christ Jesus: for ye also have suffered like things of your own countrymen, even as they *have* of the Jews:

15. Who both killed the Lord Jesus, and their own prophets, and have persecuted us; and they please not God, and are contrary to all men:

16. Forbidding us to speak to the Gĕn'tīleṣ that they might be saved, to fill up their sins always: for the wrath is come upon them to the uttermost.

17. But we, brethren, being taken from you for a short time in presence, not in heart, endeavored the more abundantly to see your face with great desire.

18. Wherefore we would have come unto you, even I Paul, once and again; but Satan hindered us.

19. For what *is* our hope, or joy, or crown of rejoicing? *Are* not even ye in the presence of our Lord Jesus Christ at his coming?

20. For ye are our glory and joy.

CHAPTER THREE

Wherefore when we could no longer forbear, we thought it good to be left at Athens alone;

2. And sent Tĭ-mō'thē-ŭs, our brother, and minister of God, and our fellow laborer in the gospel of Christ, to establish you, and to comfort you concerning your faith:

3. That no man should be moved by these afflictions: for yourselves know that we are appointed thereunto.

4. For verily, when we were with you, we told you before that we should suffer tribulation; even as it came to pass, and ye know.

5. For this cause, when I could no longer forbear, I sent to know your faith, lest by some means the tempter have tempted you, and our labor be in vain.

6. But now when Tĭ-mō'thē-ŭs came from you unto us, and brought us good tidings of your faith and charity, and that ye have good remembrance of us always, desiring greatly to see us, as we also *to see* you:

7. Therefore, brethren, we were comforted over you in all our affliction and distress by your faith:

8. For now we live, if ye stand fast in the Lord.

9. For what thanks can we render to God again for you, for all the joy wherewith we joy for your sakes before our God;

10. Night and day praying exceedingly that we might see your face, and might perfect that which is lacking in your faith?

11. Now God himself and our Father, and our Lord Jesus Christ, direct our way unto you.

12. And the Lord make you to increase and abound in love one toward another, and toward all *men*, even as we *do* toward you:

13. To the end he may stablish your hearts unblamable in holiness before God, even our Father, at the coming of our Lord Jesus Christ with all his saints.

CHAPTER FOUR

Furthermore then we beseech you, brethren, and exhort *you* by the Lord Jesus, that as ye have received of us how ye ought to walk and to please God, *so* ye would abound more and more.

2. For ye know what commandments we gave you by the Lord Jesus.

3. For this is the will of God, *even* your sanctification, that ye should abstain from fornication:

4. That every one of you should know how to possess his vessel in sanctification and honor;

5. Not in the lust of concupiscence, even as the Gĕn'tīlȩs which know not God:

6. That no *man* go beyond and defraud his brother in *any* matter: because that the Lord *is* the avenger of all such, as we also have forewarned you and testified.

7. For God hath not called us unto uncleanness, but unto holiness.

8. He therefore that despiseth, despiseth not man, but God, who hath also given unto us his Holy Spirit.

9. But as touching brotherly love ye need not that I write unto you: for ye yourselves are taught of God to love one another.

10. And indeed ye do it toward all the brethren which are in all Macedonia: but we beseech you, brethren, that ye increase more and more;

11. And that ye study to be quiet, and to do your own business, and to work with your own hands, as we commanded you;

12. That ye may walk honestly toward them that are without, and *that* ye may lack of nothing.

13. But I would not have you to be ignorant, brethren, concerning them which are asleep, that ye sorrow not, even as others which have no hope.

14. For if we believe that Jesus died and rose again, even so them also which sleep in Jesus will God bring with him.

15. For this we say unto you by the word of the Lord, that we which are alive *and* remain unto the coming of the Lord shall not prevent them which are asleep.

16. For the Lord himself shall descend from heaven with a shout, with the voice of the archangel, and with the trump of God: and the dead in Christ shall rise first:

17. Then we which are alive *and* remain shall be caught up together with them in the clouds, to meet the Lord in the air: and so shall we ever be with the Lord.

18. Wherefore comfort one another with these words.

CHAPTER FIVE

But of the times and the seasons, brethren, ye have no need that I write unto you.

2. For yourselves know perfectly that the day of the Lord so cometh as a thief in the night.

3. For when they shall say, Peace and safety; then sudden destruction cometh upon them, as travail upon a woman with child; and they shall not escape.

4. But ye, brethren, are not in darkness, that that day should overtake you as a thief.

5. Ye are all the children of light, and the children of the day: we are not of the night, nor of darkness.

6. Therefore let us not sleep, as *do* others; but let us watch and be sober.

7. For they that sleep sleep in the night; and they that be drunken are drunken in the night.

8. But let us, who are of the day, be sober, putting on the breastplate of faith and love; and for a helmet, the hope of salvation.

9. For God hath not appointed us to wrath, but to obtain salvation by our Lord Jesus Christ,

10. Who died for us, that, whether we wake or sleep, we should live together with him.

11. Wherefore comfort yourselves together, and edify one another, even as also ye do.

12. And we beseech you, brethren, to know them which labor among you, and are over you in the Lord, and admonish you;

13. And to esteem them very highly in love for their work's sake. *And* be at peace among yourselves.

14. Now we exhort you, brethren, warn them that are unruly, comfort the feebleminded, support the weak, be patient toward all *men*.

15. See that none render evil for evil unto any *man*; but ever follow that which is good, both among yourselves, and to all *men*.

16. Rejoice evermore.

17. Pray without ceasing.

18. In every thing give thanks: for this is the will of God in Christ Jesus concerning you.

19. Quench not the Spirit.

20. Despise not prophesyings.

21. Prove all things; hold fast that which is good.

22. Abstain from all appearance of evil.

23. And the very God of peace sanctify you wholly; and *I pray God* your whole spirit and soul and body be preserved blameless unto the coming of our Lord Jesus Christ.

24. Faithful *is* he that calleth you, who also will do *it*.

25. Brethren, pray for us.

26. Greet all the brethren with a holy kiss.

27. I charge you by the Lord, that this epistle be read unto all the holy brethren.

28. The grace of our Lord Jesus Christ *be* with you. Amen.

2 THESSALONIANS

CHAPTER ONE

Paul, and Sĭl-vā'nŭs, and Tĭ-mō'thē-ŭs, unto the church of the Thĕs'sȧ-lō'nĭ-ăns in God our Father and the Lord Jesus Christ:

2. Grace unto you, and peace, from God our Father and the Lord Jesus Christ.

3. We are bound to thank God always for you, brethren, as it is meet, because that your faith groweth exceedingly, and the charity of every one of you all toward each other aboundeth;

4. So that we ourselves glory in you in the churches of God, for your patience and faith in all your persecutions and tribulations that ye endure:

5. *Which is* a manifest token of the righteous judgment of God, that ye may be counted worthy of the kingdom of God, for which ye also suffer:

6. Seeing *it is* a righteous thing with God to recompense tribulation to them that trouble you;

7. And to you who are troubled rest with us, when the Lord Jesus shall be revealed from heaven with his mighty angels,

8. In flaming fire taking vengeance on them that know not God, and that obey not the gospel of our Lord Jesus Christ:

9. Who shall be punished with everlasting destruction from the presence of the Lord, and from the glory of his power;

10. When he shall come to be glorified in his saints, and to be admired in all them that believe (because our testimony among you was believed) in that day.

11. Wherefore also we pray always for you, that our God would count you worthy of *this* calling, and fulfil all the good pleasure of *his* goodness, and the work of faith with power:

12. That the name of our Lord Jesus Christ may be glorified in you, and ye in him, according to the grace of our God and the Lord Jesus Christ.

CHAPTER TWO

Now we beseech you, brethren, by the coming of our Lord Jesus Christ, and *by* our gathering together unto him,

2. That ye be not soon shaken in mind, or be troubled, neither by spirit, nor by word, nor by letter as from us, as that the day of Christ is at hand.

3. Let no man deceive you by any means: for *that day shall not come*, except there come a falling away first, and that man of sin be revealed, the son of perdition;

4. Who opposeth and exalteth himself above all that is called God, or that is worshipped; so that he as God sitteth in the temple of God, showing himself that he is God.

5. Remember ye not, that, when I was yet with you, I told you these things?

6. And now ye know what withholdeth that he might be revealed in his time.

7. For the mystery of iniquity doth already work: only he who now letteth *will let*, until he be taken out of the way.

8. And then shall that Wicked be revealed, whom the Lord shall consume with the spirit of his mouth, and shall destroy with the brightness of his coming:

9. *Even him*, whose coming is after the working of Satan with all power and signs and lying wonders,

10. And with all deceivableness of unrighteousness in them that perish; because they received not the love of the truth, that they might be saved.

11. And for this cause God shall send them strong delusion, that they should believe a lie:

12. That they all might be damned who believed not the truth, but had pleasure in unrighteousness.

13. But we are bound to give thanks always to God for you, brethren beloved of the Lord, because God hath from the beginning chosen you to salvation through sanctification of the Spirit and belief of the truth:

14. Whereunto he called you by our gospel, to the obtaining of the glory of our Lord Jesus Christ.

15. Therefore, brethren, stand fast, and hold the traditions which ye have been taught, whether by word, or our epistle.

16. Now our Lord Jesus Christ himself, and God, even our Father, which hath loved us, and hath given *us* everlasting consolation and good hope through grace,

17. Comfort your hearts, and stablish you in every good word and work.

CHAPTER THREE

Finally, brethren, pray for us, that the word of the Lord may have *free* course, and be glorified, even as *it is* with you:

2. And that we may be delivered from unreasonable and wicked men: for all *men* have not faith.

3. But the Lord is faithful, who shall stablish you, and keep *you* from evil.

4. And we have confidence in the Lord touching you, that ye both do and will do the things which we command you.

5. And the Lord direct your hearts into the love of God, and into the patient waiting for Christ.

6. Now we command you, brethren, in the name of our Lord Jesus Christ, that ye withdraw yourselves from every brother that walketh disorderly, and not after the tradition which he received of us.

7. For yourselves know how ye ought to follow us: for we behaved not ourselves disorderly among you;

8. Neither did we eat any man's bread for nought; but wrought with labor and travail night and day, that we might not be chargeable to any of you:

9. Not because we have not power, but to make ourselves an ensample unto you to follow us.

10. For even when we were with you, this we commanded you, that if any would not work, neither should he eat.

11. For we hear that there are some which walk among you disorderly, working not at all, but are busybodies.

12. Now them that are such we command and exhort by our Lord Jesus Christ, that with quietness they work, and eat their own bread.

13. But ye, brethren, be not weary in well doing.

14. And if any man obey not our word by this epistle, note that man, and have no company with him, that he may be ashamed.

15. Yet count *him* not as an enemy, but admonish *him* as a brother.

16. Now the Lord of peace himself give you peace always by all means. The Lord *be* with you all.

17. The salutation of Paul with mine own hand, which is the token in every epistle: so I write.

18. The grace of our Lord Jesus Christ *be* with you all. Amen.

GALATIANS

CHAPTER ONE

Paul, an apostle, (not of men, neither by man, but by Jesus Christ, and God the Father, who raised him from the
dead;)

2. And all the brethren which are with me, unto the
churches of Gȧ-lā'ṭĭ-ȧ:

3. Grace *be* to you, and peace, from God the Father, and
from our Lord Jesus Christ,

4. Who gave himself for our sins, that he might deliver us
from this present evil world, according to the will of God
and our Father:

5. To whom *be* glory for ever and ever. Amen.

6. I marvel that ye are so soon removed from him that
called you into the grace of Christ unto another gospel:

7. Which is not another; but there be some that trouble
you, and would pervert the gospel of Christ.

8. But though we, or an angel from heaven, preach any other gospel unto you than that which we have preached unto you, let him be accursed.

9. As we said before, so say I now again, If any *man* preach any other gospel unto you than that ye have received, let him be accursed.

10. For do I now persuade men, or God? or do I seek to please men? for if I yet pleased men, I should not be the servant of Christ.

11. But I certify you, brethren, that the gospel which was preached of me is not after man.

12. For I neither received it of man, neither was I taught *it*, but by the revelation of Jesus Christ.

13. For ye have heard of my conversation in time past in the Jews' religion, how that beyond measure I persecuted the church of God, and wasted it:

14. And profited in the Jews' religion above many my equals in mine own nation, being more exceedingly zealous of the traditions of my fathers.

15. But when it pleased God, who separated me from my mother's womb, and called *me* by his grace,

16. To reveal his Son in me, that I might preach him among the heathen; immediately I conferred not with flesh and blood:

17. Neither went I up to Jerusalem to them which were apostles before me; but I went into Arabia, and returned again unto Damascus.

18. Then after three years I went up to Jerusalem to see Peter, and abode with him fifteen days.

19. But other of the apostles saw I none, save James the Lord's brother.

20. Now the things which I write unto you, behold, before God, I lie not.

21. Afterward I came into the regions of Syria and Çĭ-lĭ'çĭ-à;

22. And was unknown by face unto the churches of Judea which were in Christ:

23. But they had heard only, That he which persecuted us in times past now preacheth the faith which once he destroyed.

24. And they glorified God in me.

CHAPTER TWO

Then fourteen years after I went up again to Jerusalem with Barnabas, and took Titus with *me* also.

2. And I went up by revelation, and communicated unto them that gospel which I preach among the Gĕn'tīleṣ, but privately to them which were of reputation, lest by any means I should run, or had run, in vain.

3. But neither Titus, who was with me, being a Greek, was compelled to be circumcised:

4. And that because of false brethren unawares brought in, who came in privily to spy out our liberty which we have in Christ Jesus, that they might bring us into bondage:

5. To whom we gave place by subjection, no, not for an hour; that the truth of the gospel might continue with you.

6. But of those who seemed to be somewhat, (whatsoever they were, it maketh no matter to me: God accepteth no man's person:) for they who seemed *to be somewhat* in conference added nothing to me:

7. But contrariwise, when they saw that the gospel of the uncircumcision was committed unto me, as *the gospel* of the circumcision *was* unto Peter;

8. (For he that wrought effectually in Peter to the apostleship of the circumcision, the same was mighty in me toward the Gĕn'tīleṣ;)

9. And when James, Çē'phăs, and John, who seemed to be pillars, perceived the grace that was given unto me, they gave to me and Barnabas the right hands of fellowship; that we *should go* unto the heathen, and they unto the circumcision.

10. Only *they would* that we should remember the poor; the same which I also was forward to do.

11. But when Peter was come to Ăn'tĭ-ŏεh, I withstood him to the face, because he was to be blamed.

12. For before that certain came from James, he did eat with the Gĕn'tīleṣ: but when they were come, he withdrew and separated himself, fearing them which were of the circumcision.

13. And the other Jews dissembled likewise with him; insomuch that Barnabas also was carried away with their dissimulation.

14. But when I saw that they walked not uprightly according to the truth of the gospel, I said unto Peter before *them* all, If thou, being a Jew, livest after the manner of Gĕn'tīleṣ, and not as do the Jews, why compellest thou the Gĕn'tīleṣ to live as do the Jews?

15. We *who are* Jews by nature, and not sinners of the Gĕn'tīlẹs,

16. Knowing that a man is not justified by the works of the law, but by the faith of Jesus Christ, even we have believed in Jesus Christ, that we might be justified by the faith of Christ, and not by the works of the law: for by the works of the law shall no flesh be justified.

17. But if, while we seek to be justified by Christ, we ourselves also are found sinners, *is* therefore Christ the minister of sin? God forbid.

18. For if I build again the things which I destroyed, I make myself a transgressor.

19. For I through the law am dead to the law, that I might live unto God.

20. I am crucified with Christ: nevertheless I live; yet not I, but Christ liveth in me: and the life which I now live in the flesh I live by the faith of the Son of God, who loved me, and gave himself for me.

21. I do not frustrate the grace of God: for if righteousness *come* by the law, then Christ is dead in vain.

CHAPTER THREE

O foolish Gà-lā'ţiăns, who hath bewitched you, that ye should not obey the truth, before whose eyes Jesus Christ hath been evidently set forth, crucified among you?

2. This only would I learn of you, Received ye the Spirit by the works of the law, or by the hearing of faith?

3. Are ye so foolish? having begun in the Spirit, are ye now made perfect by the flesh?

4. Have ye suffered so many things in vain? if *it be* yet in vain.

5. He therefore that ministereth to you the Spirit, and worketh miracles among you, *doeth he it* by the works of the law, or by the hearing of faith?

6. Even as Abraham believed God, and it was accounted to him for righteousness.

7. Know ye therefore that they which are of faith, the same are the children of Abraham.

8. And the Scripture, foreseeing that God would justify the heathen through faith, preached before the gospel unto Abraham, *saying*, In thee shall all nations be blessed.

9. So then they which be of faith are blessed with faithful Abraham.

10. For as many as are of the works of the law are under the curse: for it is written, Cursed *is* every one that continueth not in all things which are written in the book of the law to do them.

11. But that no man is justified by the law in the sight of God, *it is* evident: for, The just shall live by faith.

12. And the law is not of faith: but, The man that doeth them shall live in them.

13. Christ hath redeemed us from the curse of the law, being made a curse for us: for it is written, Cursed *is* every one that hangeth on a tree:

14. That the blessing of Abraham might come on the Gĕn'tīleṣ through Jesus Christ; that we might receive the promise of the Spirit through faith.

15. Brethren, I speak after the manner of men; Though *it be* but a man's covenant, yet *if it be* confirmed, no man disannulleth, or addeth thereto.

16. Now to Abraham and his seed were the promises made. He saith not, And to seeds, as of many; but as of one, And to thy seed, which is Christ.

17. And this I say, *that* the covenant, that was confirmed before of God in Christ, the law, which was four hundred and thirty years after, cannot disannul, that it should make the promise of none effect.

18. For if the inheritance *be* of the law, *it is* no more of promise: but God gave *it* to Abraham by promise.

19. Wherefore then *serveth* the law? It was added because of transgressions, till the seed should come to whom the promise was made; *and it was* ordained by angels in the hand of a mediator.

20. Now a mediator is not *a mediator* of one, but God is one.

21. *Is* the law then against the promises of God? God forbid: for if there had been a law given which could have given life, verily righteousness should have been by the law.

22. But the Scripture hath concluded all under sin, that the promise by faith of Jesus Christ might be given to them that believe.

23. But before faith came, we were kept under the law, shut up unto the faith which should afterward be revealed.

24. Wherefore the law was our schoolmaster *to bring us* unto Christ, that we might be justified by faith.

25. But after that faith is come, we are no longer under a schoolmaster.

26. For ye are all the children of God by faith in Christ Jesus.

27. For as many of you as have been baptized into Christ have put on Christ.

28. There is neither Jew nor Greek, there is neither bond nor free, there is neither male nor female: for ye are all one in Christ Jesus.

29. And if ye *be* Christ's, then are ye Abraham's seed, and heirs according to the promise.

CHAPTER FOUR

Now I say, *That* the heir, as long as he is a child, differeth nothing from a servant, though he be lord of all;

2. But is under tutors and governors until the time appointed of the father.

3. Even so we, when we were children, were in bondage under the elements of the world:

4. But when the fulness of the time was come, God sent forth his Son, made of a woman, made under the law,

5. To redeem them that were under the law, that we might receive the adoption of sons.

6. And because ye are sons, God hath sent forth the Spirit of his Son into your hearts, crying, Abba, Father.

7. Wherefore thou art no more a servant, but a son; and if a son, then an heir of God through Christ.

8. Howbeit then, when ye knew not God, ye did service unto them which by nature are no gods.

9. But now, after that ye have known God, or rather are known of God, how turn ye again to the weak and beggarly elements, whereunto ye desire again to be in bondage?

10. Ye observe days, and months, and times, and years.

11. I am afraid of you, lest I have bestowed upon you labor in vain.

12. Brethren, I beseech you, be as I *am*; for I *am* as ye *are*: ye have not injured me at all.

13. Ye know how through infirmity of the flesh I preached the gospel unto you at the first.

14. And my temptation which was in my flesh ye despised not, nor rejected; but received me as an angel of God, *even* as Christ Jesus.

15. Where is then the blessedness ye spake of? for I bear you record, that, if *it had been* possible, ye would have plucked out your own eyes, and have given them to me.

16. Am I therefore become your enemy, because I tell you the truth?

17. They zealously affect you, *but* not well; yea, they would exclude you, that ye might affect them.

18. But *it is* good to be zealously affected always in *a* good *thing*, and not only when I am present with you.

19. My little children, of whom I travail in birth again until Christ be formed in you,

20. I desire to be present with you now, and to change my voice; for I stand in doubt of you.

21. Tell me, ye that desire to be under the law, do ye not hear the law?

22. For it is written, that Abraham had two sons, the one by a bondmaid, the other by a free woman.

23. But he *who was* of the bondwoman was born after the flesh; but he of the free woman *was* by promise.

24. Which things are an allegory: for these are the two covenants; the one from the mount Sī'naī, which gendereth to bondage, which is Ā'gär.

25. For this Ā'gär is mount Sī'naī in Arabia, and answereth to Jerusalem which now is, and is in bondage with her children.

26. But Jerusalem which is above is free, which is the mother of us all.

27. For it is written, Rejoice, thou barren that bearest not; break forth and cry, thou that travailest not: for the desolate hath many more children than she which hath a husband.

28. Now we, brethren, as Isaac was, are the children of promise.

29. But as then he that was born after the flesh persecuted him *that was born* after the Spirit, even so *it is* now.

30. Nevertheless what saith the Scripture? Cast out the bondwoman and her son: for the son of the bondwoman shall not be heir with the son of the free woman.

31. So then, brethren, we are not children of the bond-woman, but of the free.

CHAPTER FIVE

Stand fast therefore in the liberty wherewith Christ hath made us free, and be not entangled again with the yoke of bondage.

2. Behold, I Paul say unto you, that if ye be circumcised, Christ shall profit you nothing.

3. For I testify again to every man that is circumcised, that he is a debtor to do the whole law.

4. Christ is become of no effect unto you, whosoever of you are justified by the law; ye are fallen from grace.

5. For we through the Spirit wait for the hope of righteousness by faith.

6. For in Jesus Christ neither circumcision availeth any thing, nor uncircumcision; but faith which worketh by love.

7. Ye did run well; who did hinder you that ye should not obey the truth?

8. This persuasion *cometh* not of him that calleth you.

9. A little leaven leaveneth the whole lump.

10. I have confidence in you through the Lord, that ye will be none otherwise minded: but he that troubleth you shall bear his judgment, whosoever he be.

11. And I, brethren, if I yet preach circumcision, why do I yet suffer persecution? then is the offense of the cross ceased.

12. I would they were even cut off which trouble you.

13. For, brethren, ye have been called unto liberty; only *use* not liberty for an occasion to the flesh, but by love serve one another.

14. For all the law is fulfilled in one word, *even* in this; Thou shalt love thy neighbor as thyself.

15. But if ye bite and devour one another, take heed that ye be not consumed one of another.

16. *This* I say then, Walk in the Spirit, and ye shall not fulfil the lust of the flesh.

17. For the flesh lusteth against the Spirit, and the Spirit against the flesh: and these are contrary the one to the other; so that ye cannot do the things that ye would.

18. But if ye be led of the Spirit, ye are not under the law.

19. Now the works of the flesh are manifest, which are *these*, Adultery, fornication, uncleanness, lasciviousness,

20. Idolatry, witchcraft, hatred, variance, emulations, wrath, strife, seditions, heresies,

21. Envyings, murders, drunkenness, revelings, and such like: of the which I tell you before, as I have also told *you* in time past, that they which do such things shall not inherit the kingdom of God.

22. But the fruit of the Spirit is love, joy, peace, long-suffering, gentleness, goodness, faith,

23. Meekness, temperance: against such there is no law.

24. And they that are Christ's have crucified the flesh with the affections and lusts.

25. If we live in the Spirit, let us also walk in the Spirit.

26. Let us not be desirous of vainglory, provoking one another, envying one another.

CHAPTER SIX

Brethren, if a man be overtaken in a fault, ye which are spiritual, restore such a one in the spirit of meekness; considering thyself, lest thou also be tempted.

2. Bear ye one another's burdens, and so fulfil the law of Christ.

3. For if a man think himself to be something, when he is nothing, he deceiveth himself.

4. But let every man prove his own work, and then shall he have rejoicing in himself alone, and not in another.

5. For every man shall bear his own burden.

6. Let him that is taught in the word communicate unto him that teacheth in all good things.

7. Be not deceived; God is not mocked: for whatsoever a man soweth, that shall he also reap.

8. For he that soweth to his flesh shall of the flesh reap corruption; but he that soweth to the Spirit shall of the Spirit reap life everlasting.

9. And let us not be weary in well doing: for in due season we shall reap, if we faint not.

10. As we have therefore opportunity, let us do good unto all *men*, especially unto them who are of the household of faith.

11. Ye see how large a letter I have written unto you with mine own hand.

12. As many as desire to make a fair show in the flesh, they constrain you to be circumcised; only lest they should suffer persecution for the cross of Christ.

13. For neither they themselves who are circumcised keep the law; but desire to have you circumcised, that they may glory in your flesh.

14. But God forbid that I should glory, save in the cross of our Lord Jesus Christ, by whom the world is crucified unto me, and I unto the world.

15. For in Christ Jesus neither circumcision availeth any thing, nor uncircumcision, but a new creature.

16. And as many as walk according to this rule, peace *be* on them, and mercy, and upon the Ĭs'rā-ĕl of God.

17. From henceforth let no man trouble me: for I bear in my body the marks of the Lord Jesus.

18. Brethren, the grace of our Lord Jesus Christ *be* with your spirit. Amen.

1 CORINTHIANS

CHAPTER ONE

Paul, called *to be* an apostle of Jesus Christ through the will of God, and Sŏs'thē-nēs̱ *our* brother,

2. Unto the church of God which is at Corinth, to them that are sanctified in Christ Jesus, called *to be* saints, with all that in every place call upon the name of Jesus Christ our Lord, both theirs and ours:

3. Grace *be* unto you, and peace, from God our Father, and *from* the Lord Jesus Christ.

4. I thank my God always on your behalf, for the grace of God which is given you by Jesus Christ;

5. That in every thing ye are enriched by him, in all utterance, and *in* all knowledge;

6. Even as the testimony of Christ was confirmed in you:

7. So that ye come behind in no gift; waiting for the coming of our Lord Jesus Christ:

8. Who shall also confirm you unto the end, *that ye may be* blameless in the day of our Lord Jesus Christ.

9. God *is* faithful, by whom ye were called unto the fellowship of his Son Jesus Christ our Lord.

10. Now I beseech you, brethren, by the name of our Lord Jesus Christ that ye all speak the same thing, and *that* there be no divisions among you; but *that* ye be perfectly joined together in the same mind and in the same judgment.

11. For it hath been declared unto me of you, my brethren, by them *which are of the house* of Chlō'ē, that there are contentions among you.

12. Now this I say, that every one of you saith, I am of Paul; and I of À-pŏl'lŏs; and I of Çē'phăs; and I of Christ.

13. Is Christ divided? was Paul crucified for you? or were ye baptized in the name of Paul?

14. I thank God that I baptized none of you, but Crĭs'pŭs and Gā'iŭs;

15. Lest any should say that I had baptized in mine own name.

16. And I baptized also the household of Stĕph'à-năs: besides, I know not whether I baptized any other.

17. For Christ sent me not to baptize, but to preach the gospel: not with wisdom of words, lest the cross of Christ should be made of none effect.

18. For the preaching of the cross is to them that perish, foolishness; but unto us which are saved, it is the power of God.

19. For it is written, I will destroy the wisdom of the wise, and will bring to nothing the understanding of the prudent.

20. Where *is* the wise? where *is* the scribe? where *is* the disputer of this world? hath not God made foolish the wisdom of this world?

21. For after that in the wisdom of God the world by wisdom knew not God, it pleased God by the foolishness of preaching to save them that believe.

22. For the Jews require a sign, and the Greeks seek after wisdom:

23. But we preach Christ crucified, unto the Jews a stumblingblock, and unto the Greeks foolishness;

24. But unto them which are called, both Jews and Greeks, Christ the power of God, and the wisdom of God.

25. Because the foolishness of God is wiser than men; and the weakness of God is stronger than men.

26. For ye see your calling, brethren, how that not many wise men after the flesh, not many mighty, not many noble, *are called*:

27. But God hath chosen the foolish things of the world to confound the wise; and God hath chosen the weak things of the world to confound the things which are mighty;

28. And base things of the world, and things which are despised, hath God chosen, *yea*, and things which are not, to bring to nought things that are:

29. That no flesh should glory in his presence.

30. But of him are ye in Christ Jesus, who of God is made unto us wisdom, and righteousness, and sanctification, and redemption:

31. That, according as it is written, He that glorieth, let him glory in the Lord.

CHAPTER TWO

And I, brethren, when I came to you, came not with excellency of speech or of wisdom, declaring unto you the testimony of God.

2. For I determined not to know any thing among you, save Jesus Christ, and him crucified.

3. And I was with you in weakness, and in fear, and in much trembling.

4. And my speech and my preaching *was* not with enticing words of man's wisdom, but in demonstration of the Spirit and of power:

5. That your faith should not stand in the wisdom of men, but in the power of God.

6. Howbeit we speak wisdom among them that are perfect: yet not the wisdom of this world, nor of the princes of this world, that come to nought:

7. But we speak the wisdom of God in a mystery, *even* the hidden *wisdom*, which God ordained before the world unto our glory;

8. Which none of the princes of this world knew: for had they known *it*, they would not have crucified the Lord of glory.

9. But as it is written, Eye hath not seen, nor ear heard, neither have entered into the heart of man, the things which God hath prepared for them that love him.

10. But God hath revealed *them* unto us by his Spirit: for the Spirit searcheth all things, yea, the deep things of God.

11. For what man knoweth the things of a man, save the spirit of man which is in him? even so the things of God knoweth no man, but the Spirit of God.

12. Now we have received, not the spirit of the world, but the Spirit which is of God; that we might know the things that are freely given to us of God.

13. Which things also we speak, not in the words which man's wisdom teacheth, but which the Holy Ghost teach-eth; comparing spiritual things with spiritual.

14. But the natural man receiveth not the things of the Spirit of God: for they are foolishness unto him: neither can he know *them*, because they are spiritually discerned.

15. But he that is spiritual judgeth all things, yet he himself is judged of no man.

16. For who hath known the mind of the Lord, that he may instruct him? But we have the mind of Christ.

CHAPTER THREE

And I, brethren, could not speak unto you as unto spiritual, but as unto carnal, *even* as unto babes in Christ.

2. I have fed you with milk, and not with meat: for hitherto ye were not able *to bear it*, neither yet now are ye able.

3. For ye are yet carnal: for whereas *there is* among you envying, and strife, and divisions, are ye not carnal, and walk as men?

4. For while one saith, I am of Paul; and another, I *am* of A-pŏl'lŏs; are ye not carnal?

5. Who then is Paul, and who *is* A-pŏl'lŏs, but ministers by whom ye believed, even as the Lord gave to every man?

6. I have planted, A-pŏl'lŏs watered; but God gave the increase.

7. So then neither is he that planteth any thing, neither he that watereth; but God that giveth the increase.

8. Now he that planteth and he that watereth are one: and every man shall receive his own reward according to his own labor.

9. For we are laborers together with God: ye are God's husbandry, *ye are* God's building.

10. According to the grace of God which is given unto me, as a wise master-builder, I have laid the foundation, and another buildeth thereon. But let every man take heed how he buildeth thereupon.

11. For other foundation can no man lay than that is laid, which is Jesus Christ.

12. Now if any man build upon this foundation gold, silver, precious stones, wood, hay, stubble;

13. Every man's work shall be made manifest: for the day shall declare it, because it shall be revealed by fire; and the fire shall try every man's work of what sort it is.

14. If any man's work abide which he hath built thereupon, he shall receive a reward.

15. If any man's work shall be burned, he shall suffer loss: but he himself shall be saved; yet so as by fire.

16. Know ye not that ye are the temple of God, and *that* the Spirit of God dwelleth in you?

17. If any man defile the temple of God, him shall God destroy; for the temple of God is holy, which *temple* ye are.

18. Let no man deceive himself. If any man among you seemeth to be wise in this world, let him become a fool, that he may be wise.

19. For the wisdom of this world is foolishness with God: for it is written, He taketh the wise in their own craftiness.

20. And again, The Lord knoweth the thoughts of the wise, that they are vain.

21. Therefore let no man glory in men: for all things are yours;

22. Whether Paul, or Ȧ-pŏl'lŏs, or Çē'phăs, or the world, or life, or death, or things present, or things to come; all are yours;

23. And ye are Christ's; and Christ *is* God's.

CHAPTER FOUR

Let a man so account of us, as of the ministers of Christ, and stewards of the mysteries of God.

2. Moreover it is required in stewards, that a man be found faithful.

3. But with me it is a very small thing that I should be judged of you, or of man's judgment: yea, I judge not mine own self.

4. For I know nothing by myself; yet am I not hereby justified: but he that judgeth me is the Lord.

5. Therefore judge nothing before the time, until the Lord come, who both will bring to light the hidden things of darkness, and will make manifest the counsels of the hearts: and then shall every man have praise of God.

6. And these things, brethren, I have in a figure transferred to myself and *to* Ȧ-pŏl'lŏs for your sakes; that ye might learn in us not to think *of men* above that which is written, that no one of you be puffed up for one against another.

7. For who maketh thee to differ *from another?* and what hast thou that thou didst not receive? now if thou didst receive *it*, why dost thou glory, as if thou hadst not received *it?*

8. Now ye are full, now ye are rich, ye have reigned as kings without us: and I would to God ye did reign, that we also might reign with you.

9. For I think that God hath set forth us the apostles last, as it were appointed to death: for we are made a spectacle unto the world, and to angels, and to men.

10. We *are* fools for Christ's sake, but ye *are* wise in Christ; we *are* weak, but ye *are* strong; ye *are* honorable, but we *are* despised.

11. Even unto this present hour we both hunger, and thirst, and are naked, and are buffeted, and have no certain dwelling place;

12. And labor, working with our own hands: being reviled, we bless; being persecuted, we suffer it:

13. Being defamed, we entreat: we are made as the filth of the world, *and are* the offscouring of all things unto this day.

14. I write not these things to shame you, but as my beloved sons I warn *you*.

15. For though ye have ten thousand instructors in Christ, yet *have ye* not many fathers: for in Christ Jesus I have begotten you through the gospel.

16. Wherefore I beseech you, be ye followers of me.

17. For this cause have I sent unto you Tĭ-mo'the-ŭs, who is my beloved son, and faithful in the Lord, who shall bring you into remembrance of my ways which be in Christ, as I teach every where in every church.

18. Now some are puffed up, as though I would not come to you.

19. But I will come to you shortly, if the Lord will, and will know, not the speech of them which are puffed up, but the power.

20. For the kingdom of God *is* not in word, but in power.

21. What will ye? shall I come unto you with a rod, or in love, and *in* the spirit of meekness?

CHAPTER FIVE

It is reported commonly *that there is* fornication among you, and such fornication as is not so much as named among the Gĕn'tīleṣ, that one should have his father's wife.

2. And ye are puffed up, and have not rather mourned, that he that hath done this deed might be taken away from among you.

3. For I verily, as absent in body, but present in spirit, have judged already, as though I were present, *concerning* him that hath so done this deed,

4. In the name of our Lord Jesus Christ, when ye are gathered together, and my spirit, with the power of our Lord Jesus Christ,

5. To deliver such a one unto Satan for the destruction of the flesh, that the spirit may be saved in the day of the Lord Jesus.

6. Your glorying *is* not good. Know ye not that a little leaven leaveneth the whole lump?

7. Purge out therefore the old leaven, that ye may be a new lump, as ye are unleavened. For even Christ our passover is sacrificed for us:

8. Therefore let us keep the feast, not with old leaven, neither with the leaven of malice and wickedness; but with the unleavened *bread* of sincerity and truth.

9. I wrote unto you in an epistle not to company with fornicators:

10. Yet not altogether with the fornicators of this world, or with the covetous, or extortioners, or with idolaters; for then must ye needs go out of the world.

11. But now I have written unto you not to keep company, if any man that is called a brother be a fornicator, or covetous, or an idolater, or a railer, or a drunkard, or an extortioner; with such a one, no, not to eat.

12. For what have I to do to judge them also that are without? do not ye judge them that are within?

13. But them that are without God judgeth. Therefore put away from among yourselves that wicked person.

CHAPTER SIX

Dare any of you, having a matter against another, go to law before the unjust, and not before the saints?

2. Do ye not know that the saints shall judge the world? and if the world shall be judged by you, are ye unworthy to judge the smallest matters?

3. Know ye not that we shall judge angels? how much more things that pertain to this life?

4. If then ye have judgments of things pertaining to this life, set them to judge who are least esteemed in the church.

5. I speak to your shame. Is it so, that there is not a wise man among you? no, not one that shall be able to judge between his brethren?

6. But brother goeth to law with brother, and that before the unbelievers.

7. Now therefore there is utterly a fault among you, because ye go to law one with another. Why do ye not rather take wrong? Why do ye not rather *suffer yourselves to* be defrauded?

8. Nay, ye do wrong, and defraud, and that *your* brethren.

9. Know ye not that the unrighteous shall not inherit the kingdom of God? Be not deceived: neither fornicators, nor idolaters, nor adulterers, nor effeminate, nor abusers of themselves with mankind,

10. Nor thieves, nor covetous, nor drunkards, nor revilers, nor extortioners, shall inherit the kingdom of God.

11. And such were some of you: but ye are washed, but ye are sanctified, but ye are justified in the name of the Lord Jesus, and by the Spirit of our God.

12. All things are lawful unto me, but all things are not expedient: all things are lawful for me, but I will not be brought under the power of any.

13. Meats for the belly, and the belly for meats: but God shall destroy both it and them. Now the body *is* not for fornication, but for the Lord; and the Lord for the body.

14. And God hath both raised up the Lord, and will also raise up us by his own power.

15. Know ye not that your bodies are the members of Christ? shall I then take the members of Christ, and make *them* the members of a harlot? God forbid.

16. What! know ye not that he which is joined to a harlot is one body? for two, saith he, shall be one flesh.

17. But he that is joined unto the Lord is one spirit.

18. Flee fornication. Every sin that a man doeth is without the body; but he that committeth fornication sinneth against his own body.

19. What! know ye not that your body is the temple of the Holy Ghost *which is* in you, which ye have of God, and ye are not your own?

20. For ye are bought with a price: therefore glorify God in your body, and in your spirit, which are God's.

CHAPTER SEVEN

Now concerning the things whereof ye wrote unto me: *It is* good for a man not to touch a woman.

2. Nevertheless, *to avoid* fornication, let every man have his own wife, and let every woman have her own husband.

3. Let the husband render unto the wife due benevolence: and likewise also the wife unto the husband.

4. The wife hath not power of her own body, but the husband: and likewise also the husband hath not power of his own body, but the wife.

5. Defraud ye not one the other, except *it be* with consent for a time, that ye may give yourselves to fasting and prayer; and come together again, that Satan tempt you not for your incontinency.

6. But I speak this by permission, *and* not of commandment.

7. For I would that all men were even as I myself. But every man hath his proper gift of God, one after this manner, and another after that.

8. I say therefore to the unmarried and widows, It is good for them if they abide even as I.

9. But if they cannot contain, let them marry: for it is better to marry than to burn.

10. And unto the married I command, *yet* not I, but the Lord, Let not the wife depart from *her* husband:

11. But and if she depart, let her remain unmarried, or be reconciled to *her* husband: and let not the husband put away *his* wife.

12. But to the rest speak I, not the Lord: If any brother hath a wife that believeth not, and she be pleased to dwell with him, let him not put her away.

13. And the woman which hath a husband that believeth not, and if he be pleased to dwell with her, let her not leave him.

14. For the unbelieving husband is sanctified by the wife, and the unbelieving wife is sanctified by the husband: else were your children unclean; but now are they holy.

15. But if the unbelieving depart, let him depart. A brother or a sister is not under bondage in such *cases:* but God hath called us to peace.

16. For what knowest thou, O wife, whether thou shalt save *thy* husband? or how knowest thou, O man, whether thou shalt save *thy* wife?

17. But as God hath distributed to every man, as the Lord hath called every one, so let him walk. And so ordain I in all churches.

18. Is any man called being circumcised? let him not become uncircumcised. Is any called in uncircumcision? let him not be circumcised.

19. Circumcision is nothing, and uncircumcision is nothing, but the keeping of the commandments of God.

20. Let every man abide in the same calling wherein he was called.

21. Art thou called *being* a servant? care not for it: but if thou mayest be made free, use *it* rather.

22. For he that is called in the Lord, *being* a servant, is the Lord's freeman: likewise also he that is called, *being* free, is Christ's servant.

23. Ye are bought with a price; be not ye the servants of men.

24. Brethren, let every man, wherein he is called, therein abide with God.

25. Now concerning virgins I have no commandment of the Lord: yet I give my judgment, as one that hath obtained mercy of the Lord to be faithful.

26. I suppose therefore that this is good for the present distress, *I say,* that *it is* good for a man so to be.

27. Art thou bound unto a wife? seek not to be loosed. Art thou loosed from a wife? seek not a wife.

28. But and if thou marry, thou hast not sinned; and if a virgin marry, she hath not sinned. Nevertheless such shall have trouble in the flesh: but I spare you.

29. But this I say, brethren, the time *is* short: it remaineth, that both they that have wives be as though they had none;

30. And they that weep, as though they wept not; and they that rejoice, as though they rejoiced not; and they that buy, as though they possessed not;

31. And they that use this world, as not abusing *it:* for the fashion of this world passeth away.

32. But I would have you without carefulness. He that is unmarried careth for the things that belong to the Lord, how he may please the Lord:

33. But he that is married careth for the things that are of the world, how he may please *his* wife.

34. There is difference *also* between a wife and a virgin. The unmarried woman careth for the things of the Lord, that she may be holy both in body and in spirit: but she that is married careth for the things of the world, how she may please *her* husband.

35. And this I speak for your own profit; not that I may cast a snare upon you, but for that which is comely, and that ye may attend upon the Lord without distraction.

36. But if any man think that he behaveth himself uncomely toward his virgin, if she pass the flower of *her* age, and need so require, let him do what he will, he sinneth not: let them marry.

37. Nevertheless he that standeth steadfast in his heart, having no necessity, but hath power over his own will, and hath so decreed in his heart that he will keep his virgin, doeth well.

38. So then he that giveth *her* in marriage doeth well; but he that giveth *her* not in marriage doeth better.

39. The wife is bound by the law as long as her husband liveth; but if her husband be dead, she is at liberty to be married to whom she will; only in the Lord.

40. But she is happier if she so abide, after my judgment: and I think also that I have the Spirit of God.

CHAPTER EIGHT

Now as touching things offered unto idols, we know that we all have knowledge. Knowledge puffeth up, but charity edifieth.

2. And if any man think that he knoweth any thing, he knoweth nothing yet as he ought to know.

3. But if any man love God, the same is known of him.

4. As concerning therefore the eating of those things that are offered in sacrifice unto idols, we know that an idol *is* nothing in the world, and that *there is* none other God but one.

5. For though there be that are called gods, whether in heaven or in earth, (as there be gods many, and lords many,)

6. But to us *there is but* one God, the Father, of whom *are* all things, and we in him; and one Lord Jesus Christ, by whom *are* all things, and we by him.

7. Howbeit *there is* not in every man that knowledge: for some with conscience of the idol unto this hour eat *it* as a thing offered unto an idol; and their conscience being weak is defiled.

8. But meat commendeth us not to God: for neither, if we eat, are we the better; neither, if we eat not, are we the worse.

9. But take heed lest by any means this liberty of yours become a stumblingblock to them that are weak.

10. For if any man see thee which hast knowledge sit at meat in the idol's temple, shall not the conscience of him which is weak be emboldened to eat those things which are offered to idols;

11. And through thy knowledge shall the weak brother perish, for whom Christ died?

12. But when ye sin so against the brethren, and wound their weak conscience, ye sin against Christ.

13. Wherefore, if meat make my brother to offend, I will eat no flesh while the world standeth, lest I make my brother to offend.

CHAPTER NINE

Am I not an apostle? am I not free? have I not seen Jesus Christ our Lord? are not ye my work in the Lord?

2. If I be not an apostle unto others, yet doubtless I am to you: for the seal of mine apostleship are ye in the Lord.

3. Mine answer to them that do examine me is this:

4. Have we not power to eat and to drink?

5. Have we not power to lead about a sister, a wife, as well as other apostles, and *as* the brethren of the Lord, and Çē'phăs?

6. Or I only and Barnabas, have not we power to forbear working?

7. Who goeth a warfare any time at his own charges? who planteth a vineyard, and eateth not of the fruit thereof? or who feedeth a flock, and eateth not of the milk of the flock?

8. Say I these things as a man? or saith not the law the same also?

9. For it is written in the law of Moses, Thou shalt not muzzle the mouth of the ox that treadeth out the corn. Doth God take care for oxen?

10. Or saith he *it* altogether for our sakes? For our sakes, no doubt, *this* is written: that he that ploweth should plow in hope; and that he that thresheth in hope should be partaker of his hope.

11. If we have sown unto you spiritual things, *is it* a great thing if we shall reap your carnal things?

12. If others be partakers of *this* power over you, *are* not we rather? Nevertheless we have not used this power; but suffer all things, lest we should hinder the gospel of Christ.

13. Do ye not know that they which minister about holy things live *of the things* of the temple? and they which wait at the altar are partakers with the altar?

14. Even so hath the Lord ordained that they which preach the gospel should live of the gospel.

15. But I have used none of these things: neither have I written these things, that it should be so done unto me: for *it were* better for me to die, than that any man should make my glorying void.

16. For though I preach the gospel, I have nothing to glory of: for necessity is laid upon me; yea, woe is unto me, if I preach not the gospel!

17. For if I do this thing willingly, I have a reward: but if against my will, a dispensation *of the gospel* is committed unto me.

18. What is my reward then? *Verily* that, when I preach the gospel, I may make the gospel of Christ without charge, that I abuse not my power in the gospel.

19. For though I be free from all *men*, yet have I made myself servant unto all, that I might gain the more.

20. And unto the Jews I became as a Jew, that I might gain the Jews; to them that are under the law, as under the law, that I might gain them that are under the law;

21. To them that are without law, as without law, (being not without law to God, but under the law to Christ,) that I might gain them that are without law.

22. To the weak became I as weak, that I might gain the weak: I am made all things to all *men*, that I might by all means save some.

23. And this I do for the gospel's sake, that I might be partaker thereof with *you*.

24. Know ye not that they which run in a race run all, but one receiveth the prize? So run, that ye may obtain.

25. And every man that striveth for the mastery is temperate in all things. Now they *do it* to obtain a corruptible crown; but we an incorruptible.

26. I therefore so run, not as uncertainly; so fight I, not as one that beateth the air:

27. But I keep under my body, and bring *it* into subjection: lest that by any means, when I have preached to others, I myself should be a castaway.

CHAPTER TEN

Moreover, brethren, I would not that ye should be ignorant, how that all our fathers were under the cloud, and all passed through the sea;

2. And were all baptized unto Moses in the cloud and in the sea;

3. And did all eat the same spiritual meat;

4. And did all drink the same spiritual drink; for they drank of that spiritual Rock that followed them: and that Rock was Christ.

5. But with many of them God was not well pleased: for they were overthrown in the wilderness.

6. Now these things were our examples, to the intent we should not lust after evil things, as they also lusted.

7. Neither be ye idolaters, as *were* some of them; as it is written, The people sat down to eat and drink, and rose up to play.

8. Neither let us commit fornication, as some of them committed, and fell in one day three and twenty thousand.

9. Neither let us tempt Christ, as some of them also tempted, and were destroyed of serpents.

10. Neither murmur ye, as some of them also murmured, and were destroyed of the destroyer.

11. Now all these things happened unto them for ensamples: and they are written for our admonition, upon whom the ends of the world are come.

12. Wherefore let him that thinketh he standeth take heed lest he fall.

13. There hath no temptation taken you but such as is common to man: but God *is* faithful, who will not suffer you to be tempted above that ye are able; but will with the temptation also make a way to escape, that ye may be able to bear *it*.

14. Wherefore, my dearly beloved, flee from idolatry.

15. I speak as to wise men; judge ye what I say.

16. The cup of blessing which we bless, is it not the communion of the blood of Christ? The bread which we break, is it not the communion of the body of Christ?

17. For we *being* many are one bread, *and* one body: for we are all partakers of that one bread.

18. Behold Ĭṣ'rā-ĕl after the flesh: are not they which eat of the sacrifices partakers of the altar?

19. What say I then? that the idol is any thing, or that which is offered in sacrifice to idols is any thing?

20. But *I say*, that the things which the Ġĕn'tīleṣ sacrifice, they sacrifice to devils, and not to God: and I would not that ye should have fellowship with devils.

21. Ye cannot drink the cup of the Lord, and the cup of devils: ye cannot be partakers of the Lord's table, and of the table of devils.

22. Do we provoke the Lord to jealousy? are we stronger than he?

23. All things are lawful for me, but all things are not expedient: all things are lawful for me, but all things edify not.

24. Let no man seek his own, but every man another's *wealth*.

25. Whatsoever is sold in the shambles, *that* eat, asking no question for conscience' sake:

26. For the earth *is* the Lord's, and the fulness thereof.

27. If any of them that believe not bid you *to a feast*, and ye be disposed to go; whatsoever is set before you, eat, asking no question for conscience' sake.

28. But if any man say unto you, This is offered in sacrifice unto idols, eat not for his sake that showed it, and for conscience' sake: for the earth *is* the Lord's, and the fulness thereof:

29. Conscience, I say, not thine own, but of the other: for why is my liberty judged of another *man's* conscience?

30. For if I by grace be a partaker, why am I evil spoken of for that for which I give thanks?

31. Whether therefore ye eat, or drink, or whatsoever ye do, do all to the glory of God.

32. Give none offense, neither to the Jews, nor to the Gĕn'tīleṣ, nor to the church of God:

33. Even as I please all *men* in all *things*, not seeking mine own profit, but the *profit* of many, that they may be saved.

CHAPTER ELEVEN

Be ye followers of me, even as I also *am* of Christ.

2. Now I praise you, brethren, that ye remember me in all things, and keep the ordinances, as I delivered *them* to you.

3. But I would have you know, that the head of every man is Christ; and the head of the woman *is* the man; and the head of Christ *is* God.

4. Every man praying or prophesying, having *his* head covered, dishonoreth his head.

5. But every woman that prayeth or prophesieth with *her* head uncovered dishonoreth her head: for that is even all one as if she were shaven.

6. For if the woman be not covered, let her also be shorn: but if it be a shame for a woman to be shorn or shaven, let her be covered.

7. For a man indeed ought not to cover *his* head, forasmuch as he is the image and glory of God: but the woman is the glory of the man.

8. For the man is not of the woman; but the woman of the man.

9. Neither was the man created for the woman; but the woman for the man.

10. For this cause ought the woman to have power on *her* head because of the angels.

11. Nevertheless neither is the man without the woman, neither the woman without the man, in the Lord.

12. For as the woman *is* of the man, even so *is* the man also by the woman; but all things of God.

13. Judge in yourselves: is it comely that a woman pray unto God uncovered?

14. Doth not even nature itself teach you, that, if a man have long hair, it is a shame unto him?

15. But if a woman have long hair, it is a glory to her: for *her* hair is given her for a covering.

16. But if any man seem to be contentious, we have no such custom, neither the churches of God.

17. Now in this that I declare *unto you* I praise *you* not, that ye come together not for the better, but for the worse.

18. For first of all, when ye come together in the church, I hear that there be divisions among you; and I partly believe it.

19. For there must be also heresies among you, that they which are approved may be made manifest among you.

20. When ye come together therefore into one place, *this* is not to eat the Lord's supper.

21. For in eating every one taketh before *other* his own supper: and one is hungry, and another is drunken.

22. What! have ye not houses to eat and to drink in? or despise ye the church of God, and shame them that have not? What shall I say to you? shall I praise you in this? I praise *you* not.

23. For I have received of the Lord that which also I delivered unto you, That the Lord Jesus, the *same* night in which he was betrayed, took bread:

24. And when he had given thanks, he brake *it*, and said, Take, eat; this is my body, which is broken for you: this do in remembrance of me.

25. After the same manner also *he took* the cup, when he had supped, saying, This cup is the new testament in my blood: this do ye, as oft as ye drink *it*, in remembrance of me.

26. For as often as ye eat this bread, and drink this cup, ye do show the Lord's death till he come.

27. Wherefore whosoever shall eat this bread, and drink *this* cup of the Lord, unworthily, shall be guilty of the body and blood of the Lord.

28. But let a man examine himself, and so let him eat of *that* bread, and drink of *that* cup.

29. For he that eateth and drinketh unworthily, eateth and drinketh damnation to himself, not discerning the Lord's body.

30. For this cause many *are* weak and sickly among you, and many sleep.

31. For if we would judge ourselves, we should not be judged.

32. But when we are judged, we are chastened of the Lord, that we should not be condemned with the world.

33. Wherefore, my brethren, when ye come together to eat, tarry one for another.

34. And if any man hunger, let him eat at home; that ye come not together unto condemnation. And the rest will I set in order when I come.

CHAPTER TWELVE

Now concerning spiritual *gifts*, brethren, I would not have you ignorant.

2. Ye know that ye were Gĕn'tīleṣ, carried away unto these dumb idols, even as ye were led.

3. Wherefore I give you to understand, that no man speaking by the Spirit of God calleth Jesus accursed: and *that* no man can say that Jesus is the Lord, but by the Holy Ghost.

4. Now there are diversities of gifts, but the same Spirit.

5. And there are differences of administrations, but the same Lord.

6. And there are diversities of operations, but it is the same God which worketh all in all.

7. But the manifestation of the Spirit is given to every man to profit withal.

8. For to one is given by the Spirit the word of wisdom; to another the word of knowledge by the same Spirit;

9. To another faith by the same Spirit; to another the gifts of healing by the same Spirit;

10. To another the working of miracles; to another prophecy; to another discerning of spirits; to another *divers* kinds of tongues; to another the interpretation of tongues:

11. But all these worketh that one and the selfsame Spirit, dividing to every man severally as he will.

12. For as the body is one, and hath many members, and all the members of that one body, being many, are one body: so also *is* Christ.

13. For by one Spirit are we all baptized into one body, whether *we be* Jews or Gĕn'tīleṣ, whether *we be* bond or free; and have been all made to drink into one Spirit.

14. For the body is not one member, but many.

15. If the foot shall say, Because I am not the hand, I am not of the body; is it therefore not of the body?

16. And if the ear shall say, Because I am not the eye, I am not of the body; is it therefore not of the body?

17. If the whole body *were* an eye, where *were* the hearing? If the whole *were* hearing, where *were* the smelling?

18. But now hath God set the members every one of them in the body, as it hath pleased him.

19. And if they were all one member, where *were* the body?

20. But now *are they* many members, yet but one body.

21. And the eye cannot say unto the hand, I have no need of thee: nor again the head to the feet, I have no need of you.

22. Nay, much more those members of the body, which seem to be more feeble, are necessary:

23. And those *members* of the body, which we think to be less honorable, upon these we bestow more abundant honor; and our uncomely *parts* have more abundant comeliness.

24. For our comely *parts* have no need: but God hath tempered the body together, having given more abundant honor to that *part* which lacked:

25. That there should be no schism in the body; but *that* the members should have the same care one for another.

26. And whether one member suffer, all the members suffer with it; or one member be honored, all the members rejoice with it.

27. Now ye are the body of Christ, and members in particular.

28. And God hath set some in the church, first apostles, secondarily prophets, thirdly teachers, after that miracles, then gifts of healings, helps, governments, diversities of tongues.

29. *Are* all apostles? *are* all prophets? *are* all teachers? *are* all workers of miracles?

30. Have all the gifts of healing? do all speak with tongues? do all interpret?

31. But covet earnestly the best gifts: and yet show I unto you a more excellent way.

CHAPTER THIRTEEN

Though I speak with the tongues of men and of angels, and have not charity, I am become *as* sounding brass, or a tinkling cymbal.

2. And though I have *the gift of* prophecy, and understand all mysteries, and all knowledge; and though I have all faith, so that I could remove mountains, and have not charity, I am nothing.

3. And though I bestow all my goods to feed *the poor*, and though I give my body to be burned, and have not charity, it profiteth me nothing.

4. Charity suffereth long, *and* is kind; charity envieth not; charity vaunteth not itself, is not puffed up,

5. Doth not behave itself unseemly, seeketh not her own, is not easily provoked, thinketh no evil;

6. Rejoiceth not in iniquity, but rejoiceth in the truth;

7. Beareth all things, believeth all things, hopeth all things, endureth all things.

8. Charity never faileth: but whether *there be* prophecies, they shall fail; whether *there be* tongues, they shall cease; whether *there be* knowledge, it shall vanish away.

9. For we know in part, and we prophesy in part.

10. But when that which is perfect is come, then that which is in part shall be done away.

11. When I was a child, I spake as a child, I understood as a child, I thought as a child: but when I became a man, I put away childish things.

12. For now we see through a glass, darkly; but then face to face: now I know in part; but then shall I know even as also I am known.

13. And now abideth faith, hope, charity, these three; but the greatest of these *is* charity.

CHAPTER FOURTEEN

Follow after charity, and desire spiritual *gifts*, but rather that ye may prophesy.

2. For he that speaketh in an *unknown* tongue speaketh not unto men, but unto God: for no man understandeth *him*; howbeit in the spirit he speaketh mysteries.

3. But he that prophesieth speaketh unto men *to* edification, and exhortation, and comfort.

4. He that speaketh in an *unknown* tongue edifieth himself; but he that prophesieth edifieth the church.

5. I would that ye all spake with tongues, but rather that ye prophesied: for greater *is* he that prophesieth than he that speaketh with tongues, except he interpret, that the church may receive edifying.

6. Now, brethren, if I come unto you speaking with tongues, what shall I profit you, except I shall speak to you either by revelation, or by knowledge, or by prophesying, or by doctrine?

7. And even things without life giving sound, whether pipe or harp, except they give a distinction in the sounds, how shall it be known what is piped or harped?

8. For if the trumpet give an uncertain sound, who shall prepare himself to the battle?

9. So likewise ye, except ye utter by the tongue words easy to be understood, how shall it be known what is spoken? for ye shall speak into the air.

10. There are, it may be, so many kinds of voices in the world, and none of them *is* without signification.

11. Therefore if I know not the meaning of the voice, I shall be unto him that speaketh a barbarian, and he that speaketh *shall be* a barbarian unto me.

12. Even so ye, forasmuch as ye are zealous of spiritual *gifts*, seek that ye may excel to the edifying of the church.

13. Wherefore let him that speaketh in an *unknown* tongue pray that he may interpret.

14. For if I pray in an *unknown* tongue, my spirit prayeth, but my understanding is unfruitful.

15. What is it then? I will pray with the spirit, and I will pray with the understanding also: I will sing with the spirit, and I will sing with the understanding also.

16. Else, when thou shalt bless with the spirit, how shall he that occupieth the room of the unlearned say Amen at thy giving of thanks, seeing he understandeth not what thou sayest?

17. For thou verily givest thanks well, but the other is not edified.

18. I thank my God, I speak with tongues more than ye all:

19. Yet in the church I had rather speak five words with my understanding, that *by my voice* I might teach others also, than ten thousand words in an *unknown* tongue.

20. Brethren, be not children in understanding: howbeit in malice be ye children, but in understanding be men.

21. In the law it is written, With *men of* other tongues and other lips will I speak unto this people; and yet for all that will they not hear me, saith the Lord.

22. Wherefore tongues are for a sign, not to them that believe, but to them that believe not: but prophesying *serveth* not for them that believe not, but for them which believe.

23. If therefore the whole church be come together into one place, and all speak with tongues, and there come in *those that are* unlearned, or unbelievers, will they not say that ye are mad?

24. But if all prophesy, and there come in one that believeth not, or *one* unlearned, he is convinced of all, he is judged of all:

25. And thus are the secrets of his heart made manifest; and so falling down on *his* face he will worship God, and report that God is in you of a truth.

26. How is it then, brethren? when ye come together, every one of you hath a psalm, hath a doctrine, hath a tongue, hath a revelation, hath an interpretation. Let all things be done unto edifying.

27. If any man speak in an *unknown* tongue, *let it be* by two, or at the most *by* three, and *that* by course; and let one interpret.

28. But if there be no interpreter, let him keep silence in the church; and let him speak to himself, and to God.

29. Let the prophets speak two or three, and let the other judge.

30. If *any thing* be revealed to another that sitteth by, let the first hold his peace.

31. For ye may all prophesy one by one, that all may learn, and all may be comforted.

32. And the spirits of the prophets are subject to the prophets.

33. For God is not *the author* of confusion, but of peace, as in all churches of the saints.

34. Let your women keep silence in the churches: for it is not permitted unto them to speak; but *they are commanded* to be under obedience, as also saith the law.

35. And if they will learn any thing, let them ask their husbands at home: for it is a shame for women to speak in the church.

36. What! came the word of God out from you? or came it unto you only?

37. If any man think himself to be a prophet, or spiritual, let him acknowledge that the things that I write unto you are the commandments of the Lord.

38. But if any man be ignorant, let him be ignorant.

39. Wherefore, brethren, covet to prophesy, and forbid not to speak with tongues.

40. Let all things be done decently and in order.

CHAPTER FIFTEEN

Moreover, brethren, I declare unto you the gospel which I preached unto you, which also ye have received, and wherein ye stand;

2. By which also ye are saved, if ye keep in memory what I preached unto you, unless ye have believed in vain.

3. For I delivered unto you first of all that which I also received, how that Christ died for our sins according to the Scriptures;

4. And that he was buried, and that he rose again the third day according to the Scriptures:

5. And that he was seen of Cē'phăs, then of the twelve:

6. After that, he was seen of above five hundred brethren at once; of whom the greater part remain unto this present, but some are fallen asleep.

7. After that, he was seen of James; then of all the apostles.

8. And last of all he was seen of me also, as of one born out of due time.

9. For I am the least of the apostles, that am not meet to be called an apostle, because I persecuted the church of God.

10. But by the grace of God I am what I am: and his grace which *was bestowed* upon me was not in vain; but I labored more abundantly than they all: yet not I, but the grace of God which was with me.

11. Therefore whether *it were* I or they, so we preach, and so ye believed.

12. Now if Christ be preached that he rose from the dead, how say some among you that there is no resurrection of the dead?

13. But if there be no resurrection of the dead, then is Christ not risen:

14. And if Christ be not risen, then *is* our preaching vain, and your faith *is* also vain.

15. Yea, and we are found false witnesses of God; because we have testified of God that he raised up Christ: whom he raised not up, if so be that the dead rise not.

16. For if the dead rise not, then is not Christ raised:

17. And if Christ be not raised, your faith *is* vain; ye are yet in your sins.

18. Then they also which are fallen asleep in Christ are perished.

19. If in this life only we have hope in Christ, we are of all men most miserable.

20. But now is Christ risen from the dead, *and* become the firstfruits of them that slept.

21. For since by man *came* death, by man *came* also the resurrection of the dead.

22. For as in Adam all die, even so in Christ shall all be made alive.

23. But every man in his own order: Christ the firstfruits; afterward they that are Christ's at his coming.

24. Then *cometh* the end, when he shall have delivered up the kingdom to God, even the Father; when he shall have put down all rule, and all authority and power.

25. For he must reign, till he hath put all enemies under his feet.

26. The last enemy *that* shall be destroyed *is* death.

27. For he hath put all things under his feet. But when he saith, All things are put under *him, it is* manifest that he is excepted, which did put all things under him.

28. And when all things shall be subdued unto him, then shall the Son also himself be subject unto him that put all things under him, that God may be all in all.

29. Else what shall they do which are baptized for the dead, if the dead rise not at all? why are they then baptized for the dead?

30. And why stand we in jeopardy every hour?

31. I protest by your rejoicing which I have in Christ Jesus our Lord, I die daily.

32. If after the manner of men I have fought with beasts at Ĕph'ē-sŭs, what advantageth it me, if the dead rise not? let us eat and drink; for to-morrow we die.

33. Be not deceived: evil communications corrupt good manners.

34. Awake to righteousness, and sin not; for some have not the knowledge of God: I speak *this* to your shame.

35. But some *man* will say, How are the dead raised up? and with what body do they come?

36. *Thou* fool, that which thou sowest is not quickened, except it die:

37. And that which thou sowest, thou sowest not that body that shall be, but bare grain, it may chance of wheat, or of some other *grain*:

38. But God giveth it a body as it hath pleased him, and to every seed his own body.

39. All flesh *is* not the same flesh: but *there is* one *kind of* flesh of men, another flesh of beasts, another of fishes, *and* another of birds.

40. *There are* also celestial bodies, and bodies terrestrial: but the glory of the celestial *is* one, and the *glory* of the terrestrial *is* another.

41. *There is* one glory of the sun, and another glory of the moon, and another glory of the stars; for *one* star differeth from *another* star in glory.

42. So also *is* the resurrection of the dead. It is sown in corruption, it is raised in incorruption:

43. It is sown in dishonor, it is raised in glory: it is sown in weakness, it is raised in power:

44. It is sown a natural body, it is raised a spiritual body. There is a natural body, and there is a spiritual body.

45. And so it is written, The first man Adam was made a living soul; the last Adam *was made* a quickening spirit.

46. Howbeit that *was* not first which is spiritual, but that which is natural; and afterward that which is spiritual.

47. The first man *is* of the earth, earthy: the second man *is* the Lord from heaven.

48. As *is* the earthy, such *are* they also that are earthy: and as *is* the heavenly, such *are* they also that are heavenly.

49. And as we have borne the image of the earthy, we shall also bear the image of the heavenly.

50. Now this I say, brethren, that flesh and blood cannot inherit the kingdom of God; neither doth corruption inherit incorruption.

51. Behold, I show you a mystery; We shall not all sleep, but we shall all be changed,

52. In a moment, in the twinkling of an eye, at the last trump: for the trumpet shall sound, and the dead shall be raised incorruptible, and we shall be changed.

53. For this corruptible must put on incorruption, and this mortal *must* put on immortality.

54. So when this corruptible shall have put on incorruption, and this mortal shall have put on immortality, then shall be brought to pass the saying that is written, Death is swallowed up in victory.

55. O death, where *is* thy sting? O grave, where *is* thy victory?

56. The sting of death *is* sin; and the strength of sin *is* the law.

57. But thanks *be* to God, which giveth us the victory through our Lord Jesus Christ.

58. Therefore, my beloved brethren, be ye steadfast, unmovable, always abounding in the work of the Lord, forasmuch as ye know that your labor is not in vain in the Lord.

CHAPTER SIXTEEN

Now concerning the collection for the saints, as I have given order to the churches of Gà-lā'tǐ-à, even so do ye.

2. Upon the first *day* of the week let every one of you lay by him in store, as *God* hath prospered him, that there be no gatherings when I come.

3. And when I come, whomsoever ye shall approve by *your* letters, them will I send to bring your liberality unto Jerusalem.

4. And if it be meet that I go also, they shall go with me.

5. Now I will come unto you, when I shall pass through Macedonia: for I do pass through Macedonia.

6. And it may be that I will abide, yea, and winter with you, that ye may bring me on my journey whithersoever I go.

7. For I will not see you now by the way; but I trust to tarry a while with you, if the Lord permit.

8. But I will tarry at Ĕph'ē-sŭs until Pĕn'tē-cŏst.

9. For a great door and effectual is opened unto me, and *there are* many adversaries.

10. Now if Tĭ-mō'thē-ŭs come, see that he may be with you without fear: for he worketh the work of the Lord, as I also *do*.

11. Let no man therefore despise him: but conduct him forth in peace, that he may come unto me: for I look for him with the brethren.

12. As touching *our* brother Ȧ-pŏl'lŏs, I greatly desired him to come unto you with the brethren: but his will was not at all to come at this time; but he will come when he shall have convenient time.

13. Watch ye, stand fast in the faith, quit you like men, be strong.

14. Let all your things be done with charity.

15. I beseech you, brethren, (ye know the house of Stĕph'ȧ-năs, that it is the firstfruits of Ȧ-chā'ȧ, and *that* they have addicted themselves to the ministry of the saints,)

16. That ye submit yourselves unto such, and to every one that helpeth with *us*, and laboreth.

17. I am glad of the coming of Stĕph'-á-näs and Fôr'tū-nā'tŭs and Á-chā'ĭ-cŭs: for that which was lacking on your part they have supplied.

18. For they have refreshed my spirit and yours: therefore acknowledge ye them that are such.

19. The churches of Asia salute you. Ăq'uĭ-lá and Priscilla salute you much in the Lord, with the church that is in their house.

20. All the brethren greet you. Greet ye one another with a holy kiss.

21. The salutation of *me* Paul with mine own hand.

22. If any man love not the Lord Jesus Christ, let him be Á-nătĥ'ē-má, Măr'ản-ătĥ'á.

23. The grace of our Lord Jesus Christ *be* with you.

24. My love *be* with you all in Christ Jesus. Amen.

2 CORINTHIANS

CHAPTER ONE

Paul, an apostle of Jesus Christ by the will of God, and Timothy *our* brother, unto the church of God which is at Corinth, with all the saints which are in all A-ϵhā'ja:

2. Grace *be* to you, and peace, from God our Father, and *from* the Lord Jesus Christ.

3. Blessed *be* God, even the Father of our Lord Jesus Christ, the Father of mercies, and the God of all comfort;

4. Who comforteth us in all our tribulation, that we may be able to comfort them which are in any trouble, by the comfort wherewith we ourselves are comforted of God.

5. For as the sufferings of Christ abound in us, so our consolation also aboundeth by Christ.

6. And whether we be afflicted, *it is* for your consolation and salvation, which is effectual in the enduring of the same sufferings which we also suffer: or whether we be comforted, *it is* for your consolation and salvation.

7. And our hope of you *is* steadfast knowing, that as ye are partakers of the sufferings, so *shall ye be* also of the consolation.

8. For we would not, brethren, have you ignorant of our trouble which came to us in Asia, that we were pressed out of measure, above strength, insomuch that we despaired even of life:

9. But we had the sentence of death in ourselves, that we should not trust in ourselves, but in God which raiseth the dead:

10. Who delivered us from so great a death, and doth deliver: in whom we trust that he will yet deliver *us;*

11. Ye also helping together by prayer for us, that for the gift *bestowed* upon us by the means of many persons thanks may be given by many on our behalf.

12. For our rejoicing is this, the testimony of our conscience, that in simplicity and godly sincerity, not with fleshly wisdom, but by the grace of God, we have had our conversation in the world, and more abundantly to youward.

13. For we write none other things unto you, than what ye read or acknowledge; and I trust ye shall acknowledge even to the end;

14. As also ye have acknowledged us in part, that we are your rejoicing, even as ye also *are* ours in the day of the Lord Jesus.

15. And in this confidence I was minded to come unto you before, that ye might have a second benefit;

16. And to pass by you into Macedonia, and to come again out of Macedonia unto you, and of you to be brought on my way toward Judea.

17. When I therefore was thus minded, did I use lightness? or the things that I purpose, do I purpose according to the flesh, that with me there should be yea, yea, and nay, nay?

18. But *as* God *is* true, our word toward you was not yea and nay.

19. For the Son of God, Jesus Christ, who was preached among you by us, *even* by me and Sĭl-vā'nŭs and Tĭ-mō'thē-ŭs, was not yea and nay, but in him was yea.

20. For all the promises of God in him *are* yea, and in him Amen, unto the glory of God by us.

21. Now he which stablisheth us with you in Christ, and hath anointed us, *is* God;

22. Who hath also sealed us, and given the earnest of the Spirit in our hearts.

23. Moreover I call God for a record upon my soul, that to spare you I came not as yet unto Corinth.

24. Not for that we have dominion over your faith, but are helpers of your joy: for by faith ye stand.

CHAPTER TWO

But I determined this with myself, that I would not come again to you in heaviness.

2. For if I make you sorry, who is he then that maketh me glad, but the same which is made sorry by me?

3. And I wrote this same unto you, lest, when I came, I should have sorrow from them of whom I ought to rejoice; having confidence in you all, that my joy is *the joy* of you all.

4. For out of much affliction and anguish of heart I wrote unto you with many tears; not that ye should be grieved, but that ye might know the love which I have more abundantly unto you.

5. But if any have caused grief, he hath not grieved me, but in part: that I may not overcharge you all.

6. Sufficient to such a man *is* this punishment, which *was inflicted* of many.

7. So that contrariwise ye *ought* rather to forgive *him*, and comfort *him*, lest perhaps such a one should be swallowed up with overmuch sorrow.

8. Wherefore I beseech you that ye would confirm *your* love toward him.

9. For to this end also did I write, that I might know the proof of you, whether ye be obedient in all things.

10. To whom ye forgive any thing, I *forgive* also: for if I forgave any thing, to whom I forgave *it*, for your sakes *forgave I it* in the person of Christ;

11. Lest Satan should get an advantage of us: for we are not ignorant of his devices.

12. Furthermore, when I came to Trō'ăs to *preach* Christ's gospel, and a door was opened unto me of the Lord,

13. I had no rest in my spirit, because I found not Titus my brother; but taking my leave of them, I went from thence into Macedonia.

14. Now thanks *be* unto God, which always causeth us to triumph in Christ, and maketh manifest the savor of his knowledge by us in every place.

15. For we are unto God a sweet savor of Christ, in them that are saved, and in them that perish:

16. To the one *we are* the savor of death unto death; and to the other the savor of life unto life. And who *is* sufficient for these things?

17. For we are not as many, which corrupt the word of God: but as of sincerity, but as of God, in the sight of God speak we in Christ.

CHAPTER THREE

Do we begin again to commend ourselves? or need we, as some *others*, epistles of commendation to you, or *letters* of commendation from you?

2. Ye are our epistle written in our hearts, known and read of all men:

3. *Forasmuch as ye are* manifestly declared to be the epistle of Christ ministered by us, written not with ink, but with the Spirit of the living God; not in tables of stone, but in fleshly tables of the heart.

4. And such trust have we through Christ to God-ward:

5. Not that we are sufficient of ourselves to think any thing as of ourselves; but our sufficiency *is* of God;

6. Who also hath made us able ministers of the new testament; not of the letter, but of the spirit: for the letter killeth, but the spirit giveth life.

7. But if the ministration of death, written *and* engraven in stones, was glorious, so that the children of Ĭṣ'rā-ĕl could not steadfastly behold the face of Moses for the glory of his countenance; which *glory* was to be done away;

8. How shall not the ministration of the spirit be rather glorious?

9. For if the ministration of condemnation *be* glory, much more doth the ministration of righteousness exceed in glory.

10. For even that which was made glorious had no glory in this respect, by reason of the glory that excelleth.

11. For if that which is done away *was* glorious, much more that which remaineth *is* glorious.

12. Seeing then that we have such hope, we use great plainness of speech:

13. And not as Moses, *which* put a veil over his face, that the children of Ĭṣ'rā-ĕl could not steadfastly look to the end of that which is abolished:

14. But their minds were blinded: for until this day remaineth the same veil untaken away in the reading of the old testament; which *veil* is done away in Christ.

15. But even unto this day, when Moses is read, the veil is upon their heart.

16. Nevertheless, when it shall turn to the Lord, the veil shall be taken away.

17. Now the Lord is that Spirit: and where the Spirit of the Lord *is*, there *is* liberty.

18. But we all, with open face beholding as in a glass the glory of the Lord, are changed into the same image from glory to glory, *even* as by the Spirit of the Lord.

CHAPTER FOUR

Therefore, seeing we have this ministry, as we have received mercy, we faint not;

2. But have renounced the hidden things of dishonesty, not walking in craftiness, nor handling the word of God deceitfully; but, by manifestation of the truth, commending ourselves to every man's conscience in the sight of God.

3. But if our gospel be hid, it is hid to them that are lost:

4. In whom the god of this world hath blinded the minds of them which believe not, lest the light of the glorious gospel of Christ, who is the image of God, should shine unto them.

5. For we preach not ourselves, but Christ Jesus the Lord; and ourselves your servants for Jesus' sake.

6. For God, who commanded the light to shine out of darkness, hath shined in our hearts, to *give* the light of the knowledge of the glory of God in the face of Jesus Christ.

7. But we have this treasure in earthen vessels, that the excellency of the power may be of God, and not of us.

8. *We are* troubled on every side, yet not distressed; *we are* perplexed, but not in despair;

9. Persecuted, but not forsaken; cast down, but not destroyed;

10. Always bearing about in the body the dying of the Lord Jesus, that the life also of Jesus might be made manifest in our body.

11. For we which live are alway delivered unto death for Jesus' sake, that the life also of Jesus might be made manifest in our mortal flesh.

12. So then death worketh in us, but life in you.

13. We having the same spirit of faith, according as it is written, I believed, and therefore have I spoken; we also believe, and therefore speak;

14. Knowing that he which raised up the Lord Jesus shall raise up us also by Jesus, and shall present *us* with you.

15. For all things *are* for your sakes, that the abundant grace might through the thanksgiving of many redound to the glory of God.

16. For which cause we faint not; but though our outward man perish, yet the inward *man* is renewed day by day.

17. For our light affliction, which is but for a moment, worketh for us a far more exceeding *and* eternal weight of glory;

18. While we look not at the things which are seen, but at the things which are not seen: for the things which are seen *are* temporal; but the things which are not seen *are* eternal.

CHAPTER FIVE

For we know that, if our earthly house of *this* tabernacle were dissolved, we have a building of God, a house not made with hands, eternal in the heavens.

2. For in this we groan, earnestly desiring to be clothed upon with our house which is from heaven:

3. If so be that being clothed we shall not be found naked.

4. For we that are in *this* tabernacle do groan, being burdened: not for that we would be unclothed, but clothed upon, that mortality might be swallowed up of life.

5. Now he that hath wrought us for the selfsame thing *is* God, who also hath given unto us the earnest of the Spirit.

6. Therefore *we are* always confident, knowing that, whilst we are at home in the body, we are absent from the Lord:

7. (For we walk by faith, not by sight:)

8. We are confident, *I say*, and willing rather to be absent from the body, and to be present with the Lord.

9. Wherefore we labor, that, whether present or absent, we may be accepted of him.

10. For we must all appear before the judgment seat of Christ; that every one may receive the things *done* in *his* body, according to that he hath done, whether *it be* good or bad.

11. Knowing therefore the terror of the Lord, we persuade men; but we are made manifest unto God; and I trust also are made manifest in your consciences.

12. For we commend not ourselves again unto you, but give you occasion to glory on our behalf, that ye may have somewhat to *answer* them which glory in appearance, and not in heart.

13. For whether we be beside ourselves, *it is* to God: or whether we be sober, *it is* for your cause.

14. For the love of Christ constraineth us; because we thus judge, that if one died for all, then were all dead:

15. And *that* he died for all, that they which live should not henceforth live unto themselves, but unto him which died for them, and rose again.

16. Wherefore henceforth know we no man after the flesh: yea, though we have known Christ after the flesh, yet now henceforth know we *him* no more.

17. Therefore if any man *be* in Christ, *he is* a new creature: old things are passed away; behold, all things are become new.

18. And all things *are* of God, who hath reconciled us to himself by Jesus Christ, and hath given to us the ministry of reconciliation;

19. To wit, that God was in Christ, reconciling the world unto himself, not imputing their trespasses unto them; and hath committed unto us the word of reconciliation.

20. Now then we are ambassadors for Christ, as though God did beseech *you* by us: we pray *you* in Christ's stead, be ye reconciled to God.

21. For he hath made him *to be* sin for us, who knew no sin; that we might be made the righteousness of God in him.

CHAPTER SIX

We then, *as* workers together *with him*, beseech *you* also that ye receive not the grace of God in vain.

2. (For he saith, I have heard thee in a time accepted, and in the day of salvation have I succored thee: behold, now *is* the accepted time; behold, now *is* the day of salvation.)

3. Giving no offense in any thing, that the ministry be not blamed:

4. But in all *things* approving ourselves as the ministers of God, in much patience, in afflictions, in necessities, in distresses,

5. In stripes, in imprisonments, in tumults, in labors, in watchings, in fastings;

6. By pureness, by knowledge, by long-suffering, by kindness, by the Holy Ghost, by love unfeigned,

7. By the word of truth, by the power of God, by the armor of righteousness on the right hand and on the left,

8. By honor and dishonor, by evil report and good report: as deceivers, and *yet* true;

9. As unknown, and *yet* well known; as dying, and, behold, we live; as chastened, and not killed;

10. As sorrowful, yet alway rejoicing; as poor, yet making many rich; as having nothing, and *yet* possessing all things.

11. O *ye* Corinthians, our mouth is open unto you, our heart is enlarged.

12. Ye are not straitened in us, but ye are straitened in your own bowels.

13. Now for a recompense in the same, (I speak as unto *my* children,) be ye also enlarged.

14. Be ye not unequally yoked together with unbelievers: for what fellowship hath righteousness with unrighteousness? and what communion hath light with darkness?

15. And what concord hath Christ with Bē'lĭ-ăl? or what part hath he that believeth with an infidel?

16. And what agreement hath the temple of God with idols? for ye are the temple of the living God; as God hath said, I will dwell in them, and walk in *them*; and I will be their God, and they shall be my people.

17. Wherefore come out from among them, and be ye separate, saith the Lord, and touch not the unclean *thing*; and I will receive you,

18. And will be a Father unto you, and ye shall be my sons and daughters, saith the Lord Almighty.

CHAPTER SEVEN

Having therefore these promises, dearly beloved, let us cleanse ourselves from all filthiness of the flesh and spirit, perfecting holiness in the fear of God.

2. Receive us; we have wronged no man, we have corrupted no man, we have defrauded no man.

3. I speak not *this* to condemn *you:* for I have said before, that ye are in our hearts to die and live with *you.*

4. Great *is* my boldness of speech toward you, great *is* my glorying of you: I am filled with comfort, I am exceeding joyful in all our tribulation.

5. For, when we were come into Macedonia, our flesh had no rest, but we were troubled on every side; without *were* fightings, within *were* fears.

6. Nevertheless God, that comforteth those that are cast down, comforted us by the coming of Titus;

7. And not by his coming only, but by the consolation wherewith he was comforted in you, when he told us your earnest desire, your mourning, your fervent mind toward me; so that I rejoiced the more.

8. For though I made you sorry with a letter, I do not repent, though I did repent: for I perceive that the same epistle hath made you sorry, though *it were* but for a season.

9. Now I rejoice, not that ye were made sorry, but that ye sorrowed to repentance: for ye were made sorry after a godly manner, that ye might receive damage by us in nothing.

10. For godly sorrow worketh repentance to salvation not to be repented of: but the sorrow of the world worketh death.

11. For behold this selfsame thing, that ye sorrowed after a godly sort, what carefulness it wrought in you, yea, *what* clearing of yourselves, yea, *what* indignation, yea, *what* fear, yea, *what* vehement desire, yea, *what* zeal, yea, *what* revenge! In all *things* ye have approved yourselves to be clear in this matter.

12. Wherefore, though I wrote unto you, *I did it* not for his cause that had done the wrong, nor for his cause that suffered wrong, but that our care for you in the sight of God might appear unto you.

13. Therefore we were comforted in your comfort: yea, and exceedingly the more joyed we for the joy of Titus, because his spirit was refreshed by you all.

14. For if I have boasted any thing to him of you, I am not ashamed; but as we spake all things to you in truth, even so our boasting, which *I made* before Titus, is found a truth.

15. And his inward affection is more abundant toward you, whilst he remembereth the obedience of you all, how with fear and trembling ye received him.

16. I rejoice therefore that I have confidence in you in all *things*.

CHAPTER EIGHT

Moreover, brethren, we do you to wit of the grace of God bestowed on the churches of Macedonia;

2. How that in a great trial of affliction, the abundance of their joy and their deep poverty abounded unto the riches of their liberality.

3. For to *their* power, I bear record, yea, and beyond *their* power *they were* willing of themselves;

4. Praying us with much entreaty that we would receive the gift, and *take upon us* the fellowship of the ministering to the saints.

5. And *this they did*, not as we hoped, but first gave their own selves to the Lord, and unto us by the will of God.

6. Insomuch that we desired Titus, that as he had begun, so he would also finish in you the same grace also.

7. Therefore, as ye abound in every *thing*, *in* faith, and utterance, and knowledge, and *in* all diligence, and *in* your love to us, *see* that ye abound in this grace also.

8. I speak not by commandment, but by occasion of the forwardness of others, and to prove the sincerity of your love.

9. For ye know the grace of our Lord Jesus Christ, that, though he was rich, yet for your sakes he became poor, that ye through his poverty might be rich.

10. And herein I give *my* advice: for this is expedient for you, who have begun before, not only to do, but also to be forward a year ago.

11. Now therefore perform the doing *of it*; that as *there was* a readiness to will, so *there may be* a performance also out of that which ye have.

12. For if there be first a willing mind, *it is* accepted according to that a man hath, *and* not according to that he hath not.

13. For *I mean* not that other men be eased, and ye burdened:

14. But by an equality, *that* now at this time your abundance *may be a supply* for their want, that their abundance also may be *a supply* for your want; that there may be equality:

15. As it is written, He that *had gathered* much had nothing over; and he that *had gathered* little had no lack.

16. But thanks *be* to God, which put the same earnest care into the heart of Titus for you.

17. For indeed he accepted the exhortation; but being more forward, of his own accord he went unto you.

18. And we have sent with him the brother, whose praise *is* in the gospel throughout all the churches;

19. And not *that* only, but who was also chosen of the churches to travel with us with this grace, which is administered by us to the glory of the same Lord, and *declaration of* your ready mind:

20. Avoiding this, that no man should blame us in this abundance which is administered by us:

21. Providing for honest things, not only in the sight of the Lord, but also in the sight of men.

22. And we have sent with them our brother, whom we have oftentimes proved diligent in many things, but now much more diligent, upon the great confidence which *I have* in you.

23. Whether *any do inquire* of Titus, *he is* my partner and fellow helper concerning you: or our brethren *be inquired of, they are* the messengers of the churches, *and* the glory of Christ.

24. Wherefore show ye to them, and before the churches, the proof of your love, and of our boasting on your behalf.

CHAPTER NINE

Fᴏʀ as touching the ministering to the saints, it is superfluous for me to write to you:

2. For I know the forwardness of your mind, for which I boast of you to them of Macedonia, that Ȧ-ϵchā'i̇ȧ was ready a year ago; and your zeal hath provoked very many.

3. Yet have I sent the brethren, lest our boasting of you should be in vain in this behalf; that, as I said, ye may be ready:

4. Lest haply if they of Macedonia come with me, and find you unprepared, we (that we say not, ye) should be ashamed in this same confident boasting.

5. Therefore I thought it necessary to exhort the brethren, that they would go before unto you, and make up beforehand your bounty, whereof ye had notice before, that the same might be ready, as *a matter of* bounty, and not as *of* covetousness.

6. But this *I say*, He which soweth sparingly shall reap also sparingly; and he which soweth bountifully shall reap also bountifully.

7. Every man according as he purposeth in his heart, *so let him give*; not grudgingly, or of necessity: for God loveth a cheerful giver.

8. And God *is* able to make all grace abound toward you; that ye, always having all sufficiency in all *things*, may abound to every good work:

9. (As it is written, He hath dispersed abroad; he hath given to the poor: his righteousness remaineth for ever.

10. Now he that ministereth seed to the sower both minister bread for *your* food, and multiply your seed sown, and increase the fruits of your righteousness:)

11. Being enriched in every thing to all bountifulness, which causeth through us thanksgiving to God.

12. For the administration of this service not only supplieth the want of the saints, but is abundant also by many thanksgivings unto God;

13. While by the experiment of this ministration they glorify God for your professed subjection unto the gospel of Christ, and for *your* liberal distribution unto them, and unto all *men*;

14. And by their prayer for you, which long after you for the exceeding grace of God in you.

15. Thanks *be* unto God for his unspeakable gift.

Now I Paul myself beseech you by the meekness and gentleness of Christ, who in presence *am* base among you, but being absent bold toward you:

2. But I beseech *you*, that I may not be bold when I am present with that confidence, wherewith I think to be bold against some, which think of us as if we walked according to the flesh.

3. For though we walk in the flesh, we do not war after the flesh:

4. (For the weapons of our warfare *are* not carnal, but mighty through God to the pulling down of strongholds;)

5. Casting down imaginations, and every high thing that exalteth itself against the knowledge of God, and bringing into captivity every thought to the obedience of Christ;

6. And having in a readiness to revenge all disobedience, when your obedience is fulfilled.

7. Do ye look on things after the outward appearance? If any man trust to himself that he is Christ's, let him of himself think this again, that, as he *is* Christ's, even so *are* we Christ's.

8. For though I should boast somewhat more of our authority, which the Lord hath given us for edification, and not for your destruction, I should not be ashamed:

9. That I may not seem as if I would terrify you by letters.

10. For *his* letters, say they, *are* weighty and powerful; but *his* bodily presence *is* weak, and *his* speech contemptible.

11. Let such a one think this, that, such as we are in word by letters when we are absent, such *will we be* also in deed when we are present.

12. For we dare not make ourselves of the number, or compare ourselves with some that commend themselves: but they, measuring themselves by themselves, and comparing themselves among themselves, are not wise.

13. But we will not boast of things without *our* measure, but according to the measure of the rule which God hath distributed to us, a measure to reach even unto you.

14. For we stretch not ourselves beyond *our measure*, as though we reached not unto you; for we are come as far as to you also in *preaching* the gospel of Christ:

15. Not boasting of things without *our* measure, *that is*, of other men's labors; but having hope, when your faith is increased, that we shall be enlarged by you according to our rule abundantly,

16. To preach the gospel in the *regions* beyond you, *and* not to boast in another man's line of things made ready to our hand.

17. But he that glorieth, let him glory in the Lord.

18. For not he that commendeth himself is approved, but whom the Lord commendeth.

CHAPTER ELEVEN

Would to God ye could bear with me a little in *my* folly: and indeed bear with me.

2. For I am jealous over you with godly jealousy: for I have espoused you to one husband, that I may present *you as* a chaste virgin to Christ.

3. But I fear, lest by any means, as the serpent beguiled Eve through his subtilty, so your minds should be corrupted from the simplicity that is in Christ.

4. For if he that cometh preacheth another Jesus, whom we have not preached, or *if* ye receive another spirit, which ye have not received, or another gospel, which ye have not accepted, ye might well bear with *him.*

5. For I suppose I was not a whit behind the very chiefest apostles.

6. But though *I be* rude in speech, yet not in knowledge; but we have been thoroughly made manifest among you in all things.

7. Have I committed an offense in abasing myself that ye might be exalted, because I have preached to you the gospel of God freely?

8. I robbed other churches, taking wages *of them*, to do you service.

9. And when I was present with you, and wanted, I was chargeable to no man: for that which was lacking to me the brethren which came from Macedonia supplied: and in all *things* I have kept myself from being burdensome unto you, and *so* will I keep *myself*.

10. As the truth of Christ is in me, no man shall stop me of this boasting in the regions of Å-€hā'ịȧ.

11. Wherefore? because I love you not? God knoweth.

12. But what I do, that I will do, that I may cut off occasion from them which desire occasion; that wherein they glory, they may be found even as we.

13. For such *are* false apostles, deceitful workers, transforming themselves into the apostles of Christ.

14. And no marvel; for Satan himself is transformed into an angel of light.

15. Therefore *it is* no great thing if his ministers also be transformed as the ministers of righteousness; whose end shall be according to their works.

16. I say again, Let no man think me a fool; if otherwise, yet as a fool receive me, that I may boast myself a little.

17. That which I speak, I speak *it* not after the Lord, but as it were foolishly, in this confidence of boasting.

18. Seeing that many glory after the flesh, I will glory also.

19. For ye suffer fools gladly, seeing ye *yourselves* are wise.

20. For ye suffer, if a man bring you into bondage, if a man devour *you*, if a man take *of you*, if a man exalt himself, if a man smite you on the face.

21. I speak as concerning reproach, as though we had been weak. Howbeit, whereinsoever any is bold, (I speak foolishly,) I am bold also.

22. Are they Hebrews? so *am* I. Are they Ĭṣ'rā-ĕl-ītes? so *am* I. Are they the seed of Abraham? so *am* I.

23. Are they ministers of Christ? (I speak as a fool,) I *am* more; in labors more abundant, in stripes above measure, in prisons more frequent, in deaths oft.

24. Of the Jews five times received I forty *stripes* save one.

25. Thrice was I beaten with rods, once was I stoned, thrice I suffered shipwreck, a night and a day I have been in the deep;

26. *In* journeyings often, *in* perils of waters, *in* perils of robbers, *in* perils by *mine own* countrymen, *in* perils by the heathen, *in* perils in the city, *in* perils in the wilderness, *in* perils in the sea, *in* perils among false brethren;

27. In weariness and painfulness, in watchings often, in hunger and thirst, in fastings often, in cold and nakedness.

28. Beside those things that are without, that which cometh upon me daily, the care of all the churches.

29. Who is weak, and I am not weak? who is offended, and I burn not?

30. If I must needs glory, I will glory of the things which concern mine infirmities.

31. The God and Father of our Lord Jesus Christ, which is blessed for evermore, knoweth that I lie not.

32. In Damascus the governor under Ăr'ē-tăs the king kept the city of the Dăm'à-sçēneṣ with a garrison, desirous to apprehend me:

33. And through a window in a basket was I let down by the wall, and escaped his hands.

CHAPTER TWELVE

It is not expedient for me doubtless to glory. I will come to visions and revelations of the Lord.

2. I knew a man in Christ above fourteen years ago, (whether in the body, I cannot tell; or whether out of the body, I cannot tell: God knoweth;) such a one caught up to the third heaven.

3. And I knew such a man, (whether in the body, or out of the body, I cannot tell: God knoweth;)

4. How that he was caught up into paradise, and heard unspeakable words, which it is not lawful for a man to utter.

5. Of such a one will I glory: yet of myself I will not glory, but in mine infirmities.

6. For though I would desire to glory, I shall not be a fool; for I will say the truth: but *now* I forbear, lest any man should think of me above that which he seeth me *to be*, or *that* he heareth of me.

7. And lest I should be exalted above measure through the abundance of the revelations, there was given to me a thorn in the flesh, the messenger of Satan to buffet me, lest I should be exalted above measure.

8. For this thing I besought the Lord thrice, that it might depart from me.

9. And he said unto me, My grace is sufficient for thee: for my strength is made perfect in weakness. Most gladly therefore will I rather glory in my infirmities, that the power of Christ may rest upon me.

10. Therefore I take pleasure in infirmities, in reproaches, in necessities, in persecutions, in distresses for Christ's sake: for when I am weak, then am I strong.

11. I am become a fool in glorying; ye have compelled me: for I ought to have been commended of you: for in nothing am I behind the very chiefest apostles, though I be nothing.

12. Truly the signs of an apostle were wrought among you in all patience, in signs, and wonders, and mighty deeds.

13. For what is it wherein ye were inferior to other churches, except *it be* that I myself was not burdensome to you? forgive me this wrong.

14. Behold, the third time I am ready to come to you; and I will not be burdensome to you: for I seek not yours, but you: for the children ought not to lay up for the parents, but the parents for the children.

15. And I will very gladly spend and be spent for you; though the more abundantly I love you, the less I be loved.

16. But be it so, I did not burden you: nevertheless, being crafty, I caught you with guile.

17. Did I make a gain of you by any of them whom I sent unto you?

18. I desired Titus, and with *him* I sent a brother. Did Titus make a gain of you? walked we not in the same spirit? *walked we* not in the same steps?

19. Again, think ye that we excuse ourselves unto you? we speak before God in Christ: but *we do* all things, dearly beloved, for your edifying.

20. For I fear, lest, when I come, I shall not find you such as I would, and *that* I shall be found unto you such as ye would not: lest *there be* debates, envyings, wraths, strifes, backbitings, whisperings, swellings, tumults:

21. *And* lest, when I come again, my God will humble me among you, and *that* I shall bewail many which have sinned already, and have not repented of the uncleanness and for-nication and lasciviousness which they have committed.

CHAPTER THIRTEEN

This *is* the third *time* I am coming to you. In the mouth of two or three witnesses shall every word be established.

2. I told you before, and foretell you, as if I were present, the second time; and being absent now I write to them which heretofore have sinned, and to all other, that, if I come again, I will not spare:

3. Since ye seek a proof of Christ speaking in me, which to you-ward is not weak, but is mighty in you.

4. For though he was crucified through weakness, yet he liveth by the power of God. For we also are weak in him, but we shall live with him by the power of God toward you.

5. Examine yourselves, whether ye be in the faith; prove your own selves. Know ye not your own selves, how that Jesus Christ is in you, except ye be reprobates?

6. But I trust that ye shall know that we are not reprobates.

7. Now I pray to God that ye do no evil; not that we should appear approved, but that ye should do that which is honest, though we be as reprobates.

8. For we can do nothing against the truth, but for the truth.

9. For we are glad, when we are weak, and ye are strong: and this also we wish, *even* your perfection.

10. Therefore I write these things being absent, lest being present I should use sharpness, according to the power which the Lord hath given me to edification, and not to destruction.

11. Finally, brethren, farewell. Be perfect, be of good comfort, be of one mind, live in peace; and the God of love and peace shall be with you.

12. Greet one another with a holy kiss.

13. All the saints salute you.

14. The grace of the Lord Jesus Christ, and the love of God, and the communion of the Holy Ghost, *be* with you all. Amen.

ROMANS

CHAPTER ONE

Paul, a servant of Jesus Christ, called *to be* an apostle, separated unto the gospel of God,

2. (Which he had promised afore by his prophets in the holy Scriptures,)

3. Concerning his Son Jesus Christ our Lord, which was made of the seed of David according to the flesh;

4. And declared *to be* the Son of God with power, according to the Spirit of holiness, by the resurrection from the dead:

5. By whom we have received grace and apostleship, for obedience to the faith among all nations, for his name:

6. Among whom are ye also the called of Jesus Christ:

7. To all that be in Rome, beloved of God, called *to be* saints: Grace to you, and peace, from God our Father and the Lord Jesus Christ.

8. First, I thank my God through Jesus Christ for you all, that your faith is spoken of throughout the whole world.

9. For God is my witness, whom I serve with my spirit in the gospel of his Son, that without ceasing I make mention of you always in my prayers;

10. Making request, if by any means now at length I might have a prosperous journey by the will of God to come unto you.

11. For I long to see you, that I may impart unto you some spiritual gift, to the end ye may be established;

12. That is, that I may be comforted together with you by the mutual faith both of you and me.

13. Now I would not have you ignorant, brethren, that oftentimes I purposed to come unto you, (but was let hitherto,) that I might have some fruit among you also, even as among other Gĕn'tīleṣ.

14. I am debtor both to the Greeks, and to the Barbarians; both to the wise, and to the unwise.

15. So, as much as in me is, I am ready to preach the gospel to you that are at Rome also.

16. For I am not ashamed of the gospel of Christ: for it is the power of God unto salvation to every one that believeth; to the Jew first, and also to the Greek.

17. For therein is the righteousness of God revealed from faith to faith: as it is written, The just shall live by faith.

18. For the wrath of God is revealed from heaven against all ungodliness and unrighteousness of men, who hold the truth in unrighteousness;

19. Because that which may be known of God is manifest in them; for God hath showed *it* unto them.

20. For the invisible things of him from the creation of the world are clearly seen, being understood by the things that are made, *even* his eternal power and Godhead; so that they are without excuse:

21. Because that, when they knew God, they glorified *him* not as God, neither were thankful; but became vain in their imaginations, and their foolish heart was darkened.

22. Professing themselves to be wise, they became fools,

23. And changed the glory of the uncorruptible God into an image made like to corruptible man, and to birds, and four-footed beasts, and creeping things.

24. Wherefore God also gave them up to uncleanness, through the lusts of their own hearts, to dishonor their own bodies between themselves:

25. Who changed the truth of God into a lie, and worshipped and served the creature more than the Creator, who is blessed for ever. Amen.

26. For this cause God gave them up unto vile affections: for even their women did change the natural use into that which is against nature:

27. And likewise also the men, leaving the natural use of the woman, burned in their lust one toward another; men with men working that which is unseemly, and receiving in themselves that recompense of their error which was meet.

28. And even as they did not like to retain God in *their* knowledge, God gave them over to a reprobate mind, to do those things which are not convenient;

29. Being filled with all unrighteousness, fornication, wickedness, covetousness, maliciousness; full of envy, murder, debate, deceit, malignity; whisperers,

30. Backbiters, haters of God, despiteful, proud, boasters, inventors of evil things, disobedient to parents,

31. Without understanding, covenant-breakers, without natural affection, implacable, unmerciful:

32. Who, knowing the judgment of God, that they which commit such things are worthy of death, not only do the same, but have pleasure in them that do them.

CHAPTER TWO

Therefore thou art inexcusable, O man, whosoever thou art that judgest: for wherein thou judgest another, thou condemnest thyself; for thou that judgest doest the same things.

2. But we are sure that the judgment of God is according to truth against them which commit such things.

3. And thinkest thou this, O man, that judgest them which do such things, and doest the same, that thou shalt escape the judgment of God?

4. Or despisest thou the riches of his goodness and forbearance and long-suffering; not knowing that the goodness of God leadeth thee to repentance?

5. But, after thy hardness and impenitent heart, treasurest up unto thyself wrath against the day of wrath and revelation of the righteous judgment of God;

6. Who will render to every man according to his deeds:

7. To them who by patient continuance in well doing seek for glory and honor and immortality, eternal life:

8. But unto them that are contentious, and do not obey the truth, but obey unrighteousness, indignation and wrath,

9. Tribulation and anguish, upon every soul of man that doeth evil; of the Jew first, and also of the Ġĕn'tīle;

10. But glory, honor, and peace, to every man that worketh good; to the Jew first, and also to the Ġĕn'tīle:

11. For there is no respect of persons with God.

12. For as many as have sinned without law shall also perish without law; and as many as have sinned in the law shall be judged by the law;

13. (For not the hearers of the law *are* just before God, but the doers of the law shall be justified.

14. For when the Ġĕn'tīles, which have not the law, do by nature the things contained in the law, these, having not the law, are a law unto themselves:

15. Which show the work of the law written in their hearts, their conscience also bearing witness, and *their* thoughts the mean while accusing or else excusing one another;)

16. In the day when God shall judge the secrets of men by Jesus Christ according to my gospel.

17. Behold, thou art called a Jew, and restest in the law, and makest thy boast of God,

18. And knowest *his* will, and approvest the things that are more excellent, being instructed out of the law;

19. And art confident that thou thyself art a guide of the blind, a light of them which are in darkness,

20. An instructor of the foolish, a teacher of babes, which hast the form of knowledge and of the truth in the law.

21. Thou therefore which teachest another, teachest thou not thyself? thou that preachest a man should not steal, dost thou steal?

22. Thou that sayest a man should not commit adultery, dost thou commit adultery? thou that abhorrest idols, dost thou commit sacrilege?

23. Thou that makest thy boast of the law, through breaking the law dishonorest thou God?

24. For the name of God is blasphemed among the Gĕn'tīleṣ through you, as it is written.

25. For circumcision verily profiteth, if thou keep the law: but if thou be a breaker of the law, thy circumcision is made uncircumcision.

26. Therefore, if the uncircumcision keep the righteousness of the law, shall not his uncircumcision be counted for circumcision?

27. And shall not uncircumcision which is by nature, if it fulfil the law, judge thee, who by the letter and circumcision dost transgress the law?

28. For he is not a Jew, which is one outwardly; neither *is that* circumcision, which is outward in the flesh:

29. But he *is* a Jew, which is one inwardly; and circumcision *is that* of the heart, in the spirit, *and* not in the letter; whose praise *is* not of men, but of God.

CHAPTER THREE

What advantage then hath the Jew? or what profit *is there* of circumcision?

2. Much every way: chiefly, because that unto them were committed the oracles of God.

3. For what if some did not believe? shall their unbelief make the faith of God without effect?

4. God forbid: yea, let God be true, but every man a liar; as it is written, That thou mightest be justified in thy sayings, and mightest overcome when thou art judged.

5. But if our unrighteousness commend the righteousness of God, what shall we say? *Is* God unrighteous who taketh vengeance? (I speak as a man)

6. God forbid: for then how shall God judge the world?

7. For if the truth of God hath more abounded through my lie unto his glory; why yet am I also judged as a sinner?

8. And not *rather*, (as we be slanderously reported, and as some affirm that we say,) Let us do evil that good may come? whose damnation is just.

9. What then? are we better *than they?* No, in no wise: for we have before proved both Jews and Gĕn'tīleṣ, that they are all under sin;

10. As it is written, There is none righteous, no, not one:

11. There is none that understandeth, there is none that seeketh after God.

12. They are all gone out of the way, they are together become unprofitable; there is none that doeth good, no, not one.

13. Their throat *is* an open sepulchre; with their tongues they have used deceit; the poison of asps *is* under their lips:

14. Whose mouth *is* full of cursing and bitterness:

15. Their feet *are* swift to shed blood:

16. Destruction and misery *are* in their ways:

17. And the way of peace have they not known:

18. There is no fear of God before their eyes.

19. Now we know that what things soever the law saith, it saith to them who are under the law: that every mouth may be stopped, and all the world may become guilty before God.

20. Therefore by the deeds of the law there shall no flesh be justified in his sight: for by the law *is* the knowledge of sin.

21. But now the righteousness of God without the law is manifested, being witnessed by the law and the prophets;

22. Even the righteousness of God *which is* by faith of Jesus Christ unto all and upon all them that believe; for there is no difference:

23. For all have sinned, and come short of the glory of God;

24. Being justified freely by his grace through the redemption that is in Christ Jesus:

25. Whom God hath set forth *to be* a propitiation through faith in his blood, to declare his righteousness for the remission of sins that are past, through the forbearance of God;

26. To declare, *I say*, at this time his righteousness: that he might be just, and the justifier of him which believeth in Jesus.

27. Where *is* boasting then? It is excluded. By what law? of works? Nay; but by the law of faith.

28. Therefore we conclude that a man is justified by faith without the deeds of the law.

29. *Is he* the God of the Jews only? *is he* not also of the Gĕn'tīleṣ? Yes, of the Gĕn'tīleṣ also:

30. Seeing *it is* one God, which shall justify the circumcision by faith, and uncircumcision through faith.

31. Do we then make void the law through faith? God forbid: yea, we establish the law.

CHAPTER FOUR

What shall we say then that Abraham our father, as pertaining to the flesh, hath found?

2. For if Abraham were justified by works, he hath *whereof* to glory; but not before God.

3. For what saith the Scripture? Abraham believed God, and it was counted unto him for righteousness.

4. Now to him that worketh is the reward not reckoned of grace, but of debt.

5. But to him that worketh not, but believeth on him that justifieth the ungodly, his faith is counted for righteousness.

6. Even as David also describeth the blessedness of the man, unto whom God imputeth righteousness without works,

7. *Saying*, Blessed *are* they whose iniquities are forgiven, and whose sins are covered.

8. Blessed *is* the man to whom the Lord will not impute sin.

9. *Cometh* this blessedness then upon the circumcision *only*, or upon the uncircumcision also? for we say that faith was reckoned to Abraham for righteousness.

10. How was it then reckoned? when he was in circumcision, or in uncircumcision? Not in circumcision, but in uncircumcision.

11. And he received the sign of circumcision, a seal of the righteousness of the faith which *he had yet* being uncircumcised: that he might be the father of all them that believe, though they be not circumcised; that righteousness might be imputed unto them also:

12. And the father of circumcision to them who are not of the circumcision only, but who also walk in the steps of that faith of our father Abraham, which *he had* being *yet* uncircumcised.

13. For the promise, that he should be the heir of the world, *was* not to Abraham, or to his seed, through the law, but through the righteousness of faith.

14. For if they which are of the law *be* heirs, faith is made void, and the promise made of none effect:

15. Because the law worketh wrath: for where no law is, *there is* no transgression.

16. Therefore *it is* of faith, that *it might be* by grace; to the end the promise might be sure to all the seed; not to that only which is of the law, but to that also which is of the faith of Abraham; who is the father of us all,

17. (As it is written, I have made thee a father of many nations,) before him whom he believed, *even* God, who quickeneth the dead, and calleth those things which be not as though they were:

18. Who against hope believed in hope, that he might become the father of many nations, according to that which was spoken, So shall thy seed be.

19. And being not weak in faith, he considered not his own body now dead, when he was about a hundred years old, neither yet the deadness of Sarah's womb:

20. He staggered not at the promise of God through unbelief; but was strong in faith, giving glory to God;

21. And being fully persuaded, that what he had promised, he was able also to perform.

22. And therefore it was imputed to him for righteousness.

23. Now it was not written for his sake alone, that it was imputed to him;

24. But for us also, to whom it shall be imputed, if we believe on him that raised up Jesus our Lord from the dead;

25. Who was delivered for our offenses, and was raised again for our justification.

CHAPTER FIVE

Therefore being justified by faith, we have peace with God through our Lord Jesus Christ:

2. By whom also we have access by faith into this grace wherein we stand, and rejoice in hope of the glory of God.

3. And not only *so*, but we glory in tribulations also; knowing that tribulation worketh patience;

4. And patience, experience; and experience, hope:

5. And hope maketh not ashamed; because the love of God is shed abroad in our hearts by the Holy Ghost which is given unto us.

6. For when we were yet without strength, in due time Christ died for the ungodly.

7. For scarcely for a righteous man will one die: yet peradventure for a good man some would even dare to die.

8. But God commendeth his love toward us, in that, while we were yet sinners, Christ died for us.

9. Much more then, being now justified by his blood, we shall be saved from wrath through him.

10. For if, when we were enemies, we were reconciled to God by the death of his Son; much more, being reconciled, we shall be saved by his life.

11. And not only so, but we also joy in God through our Lord Jesus Christ, by whom we have now received the atonement.

12. Wherefore, as by one man sin entered into the world, and death by sin; and so death passed upon all men, for that all have sinned:

13. (For until the law sin was in the world: but sin is not imputed when there is no law.

ROMANS

14. Nevertheless death reigned from Adam to Moses, even over them that had not sinned after the similitude of Adam's transgression, who is the figure of him that was to come.

15. But not as the offense, so also *is* the free gift: for if through the offense of one many be dead, much more the grace of God, and the gift by grace, *which is* by one man, Jesus Christ, hath abounded unto many.

16. And not as *it was* by one that sinned, *so is* the gift: for the judgment *was* by one to condemnation, but the free gift *is* of many offenses unto justification.

17. For if by one man's offense death reigned by one; much more they which receive abundance of grace and of the gift of righteousness shall reign in life by one, Jesus Christ.)

18. Therefore, as by the offense of one *judgment came* upon all men to condemnation; even so by the righteousness of one *the free gift came* upon all men unto justification of life.

19. For as by one man's disobedience many were made sinners, so by the obedience of one shall many be made righteous.

20. Moreover the law entered, that the offense might abound. But where sin abounded, grace did much more abound:

21. That as sin hath reigned unto death, even so might grace reign through righteousness unto eternal life by Jesus Christ our Lord.

CHAPTER SIX

What shall we say then? Shall we continue in sin, that grace may abound?

2. God forbid. How shall we, that are dead to sin, live any longer therein?

3. Know ye not, that so many of us as were baptized into Jesus Christ were baptized into his death?

4. Therefore we are buried with him by baptism into death: that like as Christ was raised up from the dead by the glory of the Father, even so we also should walk in newness of life.

5. For if we have been planted together in the likeness of his death, we shall be also *in the likeness* of *his* resurrection:

6. Knowing this, that our old man is crucified with *him*, that the body of sin might be destroyed, that henceforth we should not serve sin.

7. For he that is dead is freed from sin.

8. Now if we be dead with Christ, we believe that we shall also live with him:

9. Knowing that Christ being raised from the dead dieth no more; death hath no more dominion over him.

10. For in that he died, he died unto sin once: but in that he liveth, he liveth unto God.

11. Likewise reckon ye also yourselves to be dead indeed unto sin, but alive unto God through Jesus Christ our Lord.

12. Let not sin therefore reign in your mortal body, that ye should obey it in the lusts thereof.

13. Neither yield ye your members *as* instruments of unrighteousness unto sin: but yield yourselves unto God, as those that are alive from the dead, and your members *as* instruments of righteousness unto God.

14. For sin shall not have dominion over you: for ye are not under the law, but under grace.

15. What then? shall we sin, because we are not under the law, but under grace? God forbid.

16. Know ye not, that to whom ye yield yourselves servants to obey, his servants ye are to whom ye obey; whether of sin unto death, or of obedience unto righteousness?

17. But God be thanked, that ye were the servants of sin, but ye have obeyed from the heart that form of doctrine which was delivered you.

18. Being then made free from sin, ye became the servants of righteousness.

19. I speak after the manner of men because of the infirmity of your flesh: for as ye have yielded your members servants to uncleanness and to iniquity unto iniquity; even so now yield your members servants to righteousness unto holiness.

20. For when ye were the servants of sin, ye were free from righteousness.

21. What fruit had ye then in those things whereof ye are now ashamed? for the end of those things *is* death.

22. But now being made free from sin, and become servants to God, ye have your fruit unto holiness, and the end everlasting life.

23. For the wages of sin *is* death; but the gift of God *is* eternal life through Jesus Christ our Lord.

CHAPTER SEVEN

Know ye not, brethren, (for I speak to them that know the law,) how that the law hath dominion over a man as long as he liveth?

2. For the woman which hath a husband is bound by the law to *her* husband so long as he liveth; but if the husband be dead, she is loosed from the law of *her* husband.

3. So then if, while *her* husband liveth, she be married to another man, she shall be called an adulteress: but if her husband be dead, she is free from that law; so that she is no adulteress, though she be married to another man.

4. Wherefore, my brethren, ye also are become dead to the law by the body of Christ; that ye should be married to another, *even* to him who is raised from the dead, that we should bring forth fruit unto God.

5. For when we were in the flesh, the motions of sins, which were by the law, did work in our members to bring forth fruit unto death.

6. But now we are delivered from the law, that being dead wherein we were held; that we should serve in newness of spirit, and not *in* the oldness of the letter.

7. What shall we say then? *Is* the law sin? God forbid. Nay, I had not known sin, but by the law: for I had not known lust, except the law had said, Thou shalt not covet.

8. But sin, taking occasion by the commandment, wrought in me all manner of concupiscence. For without the law sin *was* dead.

9. For I was alive without the law once: but when the commandment came, sin revived, and I died.

10. And the commandment, which *was ordained* to life, I found *to be* unto death.

11. For sin, taking occasion by the commandment, deceived me, and by it slew *me*.

12. Wherefore the law *is* holy, and the commandment holy, and just, and good.

13. Was then that which is good made death unto me? God forbid. But sin, that it might appear sin, working death in me by that which is good; that sin by the commandment might become exceeding sinful.

14. For we know that the law is spiritual: but I am carnal, sold under sin.

15. For that which I do, I allow not: for what I would, that do I not; but what I hate, that do I.

16. If then I do that which I would not, I consent unto the law that *it is* good.

17. Now then it is no more I that do it, but sin that dwelleth in me.

18. For I know that in me (that is, in my flesh,) dwelleth no good thing: for to will is present with me; but *how* to perform that which is good I find not.

19. For the good that I would, I do not: but the evil which I would not, that I do.

20. Now if I do that I would not, it is no more I that do it, but sin that dwelleth in me.

21. I find then a law, that, when I would do good, evil is present with me.

22. For I delight in the law of God after the inward man:

23. But I see another law in my members, warring against the law of my mind, and bringing me into captivity to the law of sin which is in my members.

24. O wretched man that I am! who shall deliver me from the body of this death?

25. I thank God through Jesus Christ our Lord. So then with the mind I myself serve the law of God; but with the flesh the law of sin.

CHAPTER EIGHT

There is therefore now no condemnation to them which are in Christ Jesus, who walk not after the flesh, but after the Spirit.

2. For the law of the Spirit of life in Christ Jesus hath made me free from the law of sin and death.

3. For what the law could not do, in that it was weak through the flesh, God sending his own Son in the likeness of sinful flesh, and for sin, condemned sin in the flesh:

4. That the righteousness of the law might be fulfilled in us, who walk not after the flesh, but after the Spirit.

5. For they that are after the flesh do mind the things of the flesh; but they that are after the Spirit, the things of the Spirit.

6. For to be carnally minded *is* death; but to be spiritually minded *is* life and peace.

7. Because the carnal mind *is* enmity against God: for it is not subject to the law of God, neither indeed can be.

8. So then they that are in the flesh cannot please God.

9. But ye are not in the flesh, but in the Spirit, if so be that the Spirit of God dwell in you. Now if any man have not the Spirit of Christ, he is none of his.

10. And if Christ *be* in you, the body *is* dead because of sin; but the Spirit *is* life because of righteousness.

11. But if the Spirit of him that raised up Jesus from the dead dwell in you, he that raised up Christ from the dead shall also quicken your mortal bodies by his Spirit that dwelleth in you.

12. Therefore, brethren, we are debtors, not to the flesh, to live after the flesh.

13. For if ye live after the flesh, ye shall die: but if ye through the Spirit do mortify the deeds of the body, ye shall live.

14. For as many as are led by the Spirit of God, they are the sons of God.

15. For ye have not received the spirit of bondage again to fear; but ye have received the Spirit of adoption, whereby we cry, Abba, Father.

16. The Spirit itself beareth witness with our spirit, that we are the children of God:

17. And if children, then heirs; heirs of God, and joint-heirs with Christ; if so be that we suffer with *him*, that we may be also glorified together.

18. For I reckon that the sufferings of this present time *are* not worthy *to be compared* with the glory which shall be revealed in us.

19. For the earnest expectation of the creature waiteth for the manifestation of the sons of God.

20. For the creature was made subject to vanity, not willingly, but by reason of him who hath subjected *the same* in hope;

21. Because the creature itself also shall be delivered from the bondage of corruption into the glorious liberty of the children of God.

22. For we know that the whole creation groaneth and travaileth in pain together until now.

23. And not only *they*, but ourselves also, which have the firstfruits of the Spirit, even we ourselves groan within ourselves, waiting for the adoption, *to wit*, the redemption of our body.

24. For we are saved by hope: but hope that is seen is not hope: for what a man seeth, why doth he yet hope for?

25. But if we hope for that we see not, *then* do we with patience wait for *it*.

26. Likewise the Spirit also helpeth our infirmities: for we know not what we should pray for as we ought: but the Spirit itself maketh intercession for us with groanings which cannot be uttered.

27. And he that searcheth the hearts knoweth what *is* the mind of the Spirit, because he maketh intercession for the saints according to *the will of* God.

28. And we know that all things work together for good to them that love God, to them who are the called according to *his* purpose.

29. For whom he did foreknow, he also did predestinate *to be* conformed to the image of his Son, that he might be the firstborn among many brethren.

30. Moreover, whom he did predestinate, them he also called: and whom he called, them he also justified: and whom he justified, them he also glorified.

31. What shall we then say to these things? If God *be* for us, who *can be* against us?

32. He that spared not his own Son, but delivered him up for us all, how shall he not with him also freely give us all things?

33. Who shall lay any thing to the charge of God's elect? *It is* God that justifieth.

34. Who *is* he that condemneth? *It is* Christ that died, yea rather, that is risen again, who is even at the right hand of God, who also maketh intercession for us.

35. Who shall separate us from the love of Christ? *shall* tribulation, or distress, or persecution, or famine, or nakedness, or peril, or sword?

36. As it is written, For thy sake we are killed all the day long; we are accounted as sheep for the slaughter.

37. Nay, in all these things we are more than conquerors through him that loved us.

38. For I am persuaded, that neither death, nor life, nor angels, nor principalities, nor powers, nor things present, nor things to come,

39. Nor height, nor depth, nor any other creature, shall be able to separate us from the love of God, which is in Christ Jesus our Lord.

CHAPTER NINE

I say the truth in Christ, I lie not, my conscience also bearing me witness in the Holy Ghost,

2. That I have great heaviness and continual sorrow in my heart.

3. For I could wish that myself were accursed from Christ for my brethren, my kinsmen according to the flesh:

4. Who are Ĭṣ'rā-ĕl-ītes; to whom *pertaineth* the adoption, and the glory, and the covenants, and the giving of the law, and the service *of God*, and the promises;

5. Whose *are* the fathers, and of whom as concerning the flesh Christ *came*, who is over all, God blessed for ever. Amen.

6. Not as though the word of God hath taken none effect. For they *are* not all Ĭṣ'rā-ĕl, which are of Ĭṣ'rā-ĕl:

7. Neither, because they are the seed of Abraham, *are they* all children: but, In Isaac shall thy seed be called.

8. That is, They which are the children of the flesh, these *are* not the children of God: but the children of the promise are counted for the seed.

9. For this *is* the word of promise, At this time will I come, and Sarah shall have a son.

10. And not only *this*; but when Rē-bĕc'cà also had conceived by one, *even* by our father Isaac,

11. (For *the children* being not yet born, neither having done any good or evil, that the purpose of God according to election might stand, not of works, but of him that calleth;)

12. It was said unto her, The elder shall serve the younger.

13. As it is written, Jacob have I loved, but Ē'saū have I hated.

14. What shall we say then? *Is there* unrighteousness with God? God forbid.

15. For he saith to Moses, I will have mercy on whom I will have mercy, and I will have compassion on whom I will have compassion.

16. So then *it is* not of him that willeth, nor of him that runneth, but of God that showeth mercy.

17. For the Scripture saith unto Phā'raōh, Even for this same purpose have I raised thee up, that I might show my power in thee, and that my name might be declared throughout all the earth.

18. Therefore hath he mercy on whom he will *have mercy*, and whom he will he hardeneth.

19. Thou wilt say then unto me, Why doth he yet find fault? For who hath resisted his will?

20. Nay but, O man, who art thou that repliest against God? Shall the thing formed say to him that formed *it*, Why hast thou made me thus?

21. Hath not the potter power over the clay, of the same lump to make one vessel unto honor, and another unto dishonor?

22. *What* if God, willing to show *his* wrath, and to make his power known, endured with much long-suffering the vessels of wrath fitted to destruction:

23. And that he might make known the riches of his glory on the vessels of mercy, which he had afore prepared unto glory,

24. Even us, whom he hath called, not of the Jews only, but also of the Ğĕn'tīlȩ?

25. As he saith also in Ō'ṣēe, I will call them my people, which were not my people; and her beloved, which was not beloved.

26. And it shall come to pass, *that* in the place where it was said unto them, Ye *are* not my people; there shall they be called the children of the living God.

27. Ē-ṣā'ïǎs also crieth concerning Ĭṣ'rā-ĕl, Though the number of the children of Ĭṣ'rā-ĕl be as the sand of the sea, a remnant shall be saved:

28. For he will finish the work, and cut *it* short in righteousness: because a short work will the Lord make upon the earth.

29. And as Ē-ṣā'ïǎs said before, Except the Lord of Sǎb'ā-ŏth had left us a seed, we had been as Sŏd'ō-mȧ, and been made like unto Gō-mŏr'rȧh.

30. What shall we say then? That the Ğĕn'tīlȩ, which followed not after righteousness, have attained to righteousness, even the righteousness which is of faith.

31. But Ĭṣ'rā-ĕl, which followed after the law of righteousness, hath not attained to the law of righteousness.

32. Wherefore? Because *they sought it* not by faith, but as it were by the works of the law. For they stumbled at that stumblingstone;

33. As it is written, Behold, I lay in Sī'ón a stumblingstone and rock of offense: and whosoever believeth on him shall not be ashamed.

CHAPTER TEN

Brethren, my heart's desire and prayer to God for Ĭṣ'rā-ĕl is, that they might be saved.

2. For I bear them record that they have a zeal of God, but not according to knowledge.

3. For they, being ignorant of God's righteousness, and going about to establish their own righteousness, have not submitted themselves unto the righteousness of God.

4. For Christ *is* the end of the law for righteousness to every one that believeth.

5. For Moses describeth the righteousness which is of the law, That the man which doeth those things shall live by them.

6. But the righteousness which is of faith speaketh on this wise, Say not in thine heart, Who shall ascend into heaven? (that is, to bring Christ down *from above:*)

7. Or, Who shall descend into the deep? (that is, to bring up Christ again from the dead.)

8. But what saith it? The word is nigh thee, *even* in thy mouth, and in thy heart: that is, the word of faith, which we preach;

9. That if thou shalt confess with thy mouth the Lord Jesus, and shalt believe in thine heart that God hath raised him from the dead, thou shalt be saved.

10. For with the heart man believeth unto righteousness; and with the mouth confession is made unto salvation.

11. For the Scripture saith, Whosoever believeth on him shall not be ashamed.

12. For there is no difference between the Jew and the Greek: for the same Lord over all is rich unto all that call upon him.

13. For whosoever shall call upon the name of the Lord shall be saved.

14. How then shall they call on him in whom they have not believed? and how shall they believe in him of whom

they have not heard? and how shall they hear without a
preacher?

15. And how shall they preach, except they be sent? as it is
written, How beautiful are the feet of them that preach the
gospel of peace, and bring glad tidings of good things!

16. But they have not all obeyed the gospel. For Ē-ṣā'ias
saith, Lord, who hath believed our report?

17. So then faith *cometh* by hearing, and hearing by the
word of God.

18. But I say, Have they not heard? Yes verily, their sound
went into all the earth, and their words unto the ends of
the world.

19. But I say, Did not Ĭṣ'rā-ĕl know? First Moses saith, I
will provoke you to jealousy by *them that are* no people,
and by a foolish nation I will anger you.

20. But Ē-ṣā'ias is very bold, and saith, I was found of them
that sought me not; I was made manifest unto them that
asked not after me.

21. But to Ĭṣ'rā-ĕl he saith, All day long I have stretched
forth my hands unto a disobedient and gainsaying people.

CHAPTER ELEVEN

I say then, Hath God cast away his people? God forbid. For I also am an Ĭṣ'rā-ĕl-īte, of the seed of Abraham, *of* the tribe of Benjamin.

2. God hath not cast away his people which he foreknew. Wot ye not what the Scripture saith of Ē-lī'ăs? how he maketh intercession to God against Ĭṣ'rā-ĕl, saying,

3. Lord, they have killed thy prophets, and digged down thine altars; and I am left alone, and they seek my life.

4. But what saith the answer of God unto him? I have reserved to myself seven thousand men, who have not bowed the knee to *the image of* Bā'ăl.

5. Even so then at this present time also there is a remnant according to the election of grace.

6. And if by grace, then *is it* no more of works: otherwise grace is no more grace. But if *it be* of works, then is it no more grace: otherwise work is no more work.

7. What then? Ĭṣ'rā-ĕl hath not obtained that which he seeketh for; but the election hath obtained it, and the rest were blinded

8. (According as it is written, God hath given them the spirit of slumber, eyes that they should not see, and ears that they should not hear;) unto this day.

9. And David saith, Let their table be made a snare, and a trap, and a stumblingblock, and a recompense unto them:

10. Let their eyes be darkened, that they may not see, and bow down their back alway.

11. I say then, Have they stumbled that they should fall? God forbid: but *rather* through their fall salvation *is come* unto the Gĕn'tīleş, for to provoke them to jealousy.

12. Now if the fall of them *be* the riches of the world, and the diminishing of them the riches of the Gĕn'tīleş; how much more their fulness?

13. For I speak to you Gĕn'tīleş, inasmuch as I am the apostle of the Gĕn'tīleş, I magnify mine office:

14. If by any means I may provoke to emulation *them which are* my flesh, and might save some of them.

15. For if the casting away of them *be* the reconciling of the world, what *shall* the receiving *of them be*, but life from the dead?

16. For if the firstfruit *be* holy, the lump *is* also *holy:* and if the root *be* holy, so *are* the branches.

17. And if some of the branches be broken off, and thou, being a wild olive tree, wert graffed in among them, and with them partakest of the root and fatness of the olive tree;

18. Boast not against the branches. But if thou boast, thou bearest not the root, but the root thee.

19. Thou wilt say then, The branches were broken off, that I might be graffed in.

20. Well; because of unbelief they were broken off, and thou standest by faith. Be not high-minded, but fear:

21. For if God spared not the natural branches, *take heed* lest he also spare not thee.

22. Behold therefore the goodness and severity of God: on them which fell, severity; but toward thee, goodness, if thou continue in *his* goodness: otherwise thou also shalt be cut off.

23. And they also, if they abide not still in unbelief, shall be graffed in: for God is able to graff them in again.

24. For if thou wert cut out of the olive tree which is wild by nature, and wert graffed contrary to nature into a good olive tree; how much more shall these, which be the natural *branches*, be graffed into their own olive tree?

25. For I would not, brethren, that ye should be ignorant of this mystery, lest ye should be wise in your own conceits,

that blindness in part is happened to Ĭṣ'rā-ĕl, until the fulness of the Gĕn'tīleṣ be come in.

26. And so all Ĭṣ'rā-ĕl shall be saved: as it is written, There
shall come out of Sī'ȯn the Deliverer, and shall turn away
ungodliness from Jacob:

27. For this *is* my covenant unto them, when I shall take
away their sins.

28. As concerning the gospel, *they are* enemies for your
sakes: but as touching the election, *they are* beloved for the
fathers' sakes.

29. For the gifts and calling of God *are* without repentance.

30. For as ye in times past have not believed God, yet have
now obtained mercy through their unbelief:

31. Even so have these also now not believed, that through
your mercy they also may obtain mercy.

32. For God hath concluded them all in unbelief, that he
might have mercy upon all.

33. O the depth of the riches both of the wisdom and
knowledge of God! how unsearchable *are* his judgments,
and his ways past finding out!

34. For who hath known the mind of the Lord? or who
hath been his counselor?

35. Or who hath first given to him, and it shall be recompensed unto him again?

36. For of him, and through him, and to him, *are* all things: to whom *be* glory for ever. Amen.

CHAPTER TWELVE

I beseech you therefore, brethren, by the mercies of God, that ye present your bodies a living sacrifice, holy, acceptable unto God, *which is* your reasonable service.

2. And be not conformed to this world: but be ye transformed by the renewing of your mind, that ye may prove what *is* that good, and acceptable, and perfect will of God.

3. For I say, through the grace given unto me, to every man that is among you, not to think *of himself* more highly than he ought to think; but to think soberly, according as God hath dealt to every man the measure of faith.

4. For as we have many members in one body, and all members have not the same office:

5. So we, *being* many, are one body in Christ, and every one members one-of another.

6. Having then gifts differing according to the grace that is given to us, whether prophecy, *let us prophesy* according to the proportion of faith;

7. Or ministry, *let us wait* on *our* ministering; or he that teacheth, on teaching;

8. Or he that exhorteth, on exhortation: he that giveth, *let him do it* with simplicity; he that ruleth, with diligence; he that showeth mercy, with cheerfulness.

9. *Let* love be without dissimulation. Abhor that which is evil; cleave to that which is good.

10. *Be* kindly affectioned one to another with brotherly love; in honor preferring one another;

11. Not slothful in business; fervent in spirit; serving the Lord;

12. Rejoicing in hope; patient in tribulation; continuing instant in prayer;

13. Distributing to the necessity of saints; given to hospitality.

14. Bless them which persecute you: bless, and curse not.

15. Rejoice with them that do rejoice, and weep with them that weep.

16. *Be* of the same mind one toward another. Mind not high things, but condescend to men of low estate. Be not wise in your own conceits.

17. Recompense to no man evil for evil. Provide things honest in the sight of all men.

18. If it be possible, as much as lieth in you, live peaceably with all men.

19. Dearly beloved, avenge not yourselves, but *rather* give place unto wrath: for it is written, Vengeance *is* mine; I will repay, saith the Lord.

20. Therefore if thine enemy hunger, feed him; if he thirst, give him drink: for in so doing thou shalt heap coals of fire on his head.

21. Be not overcome of evil, but overcome evil with good.

CHAPTER THIRTEEN

Let every soul be subject unto the higher powers. For there is no power but of God: the powers that be are ordained of God.

2. Whosoever therefore resisteth the power, resisteth the ordinance of God: and they that resist shall receive to themselves damnation.

3. For rulers are not a terror to good works, but to the evil. Wilt thou then not be afraid of the power? do that which is good, and thou shalt have praise of the same:

4. For he is the minister of God to thee for good. But if thou do that which is evil, be afraid; for he beareth not the sword in vain: for he is the minister of God, a revenger to *execute* wrath upon him that doeth evil.

5. Wherefore *ye* must needs be subject, not only for wrath, but also for conscience' sake.

6. For, for this cause pay ye tribute also: for they are God's ministers, attending continually upon this very thing.

7. Render therefore to all their dues: tribute to whom tribute *is due;* custom to whom custom; fear to whom fear; honor to whom honor.

8. Owe no man any thing, but to love one another: for he that loveth another hath fulfilled the law.

9. For this, Thou shalt not commit adultery, Thou shalt not kill, Thou shalt not steal, Thou shalt not bear false witness, Thou shalt not covet; and if *there be* any other commandment, it is briefly comprehended in this saying, namely, Thou shalt love thy neighbor as thyself.

10. Love worketh no ill to his neighbor: therefore love *is* the fulfilling of the law.

11. And that, knowing the time, that now *it is* high time to awake out of sleep: for now *is* our salvation nearer than when we believed.

12. The night is far spent, the day is at hand: let us therefore cast off the works of darkness, and let us put on the armor of light.

13. Let us walk honestly, as in the day; not in rioting and drunkenness, not in chambering and wantonness, not in strife and envying:

14. But put ye on the Lord Jesus Christ, and make not provision for the flesh, to *fulfil* the lusts *thereof.*

CHAPTER FOURTEEN

Him that is weak in the faith receive ye, *but* not to doubtful disputations.

2. For one believeth that he may eat all things: another, who is weak, eateth herbs.

3. Let not him that eateth despise him that eateth not; and let not him which eateth not judge him that eateth: for God hath received him.

4. Who art thou that judgest another man's servant? to his own master he standeth or falleth. Yea, he shall be holden up: for God is able to make him stand.

5. One man esteemeth one day above another: another esteemeth every day *alike*. Let every man be fully persuaded in his own mind.

6. He that regardeth the day, regardeth *it* unto the Lord; and he that regardeth not the day, to the Lord he doth not regard *it*. He that eateth, eateth to the Lord, for he giveth God thanks; and he that eateth not, to the Lord he eateth not, and giveth God thanks.

7. For none of us liveth to himself, and no man dieth to himself.

8. For whether we live, we live unto the Lord; and whether we die, we die unto the Lord: whether we live therefore, or die, we are the Lord's.

9. For to this end Christ both died, and rose, and revived, that he might be Lord both of the dead and living.

10. But why dost thou judge thy brother? or why dost thou set at nought thy brother? for we shall all stand before the judgment seat of Christ.

11. For it is written, *As* I live, saith the Lord, every knee shall bow to me, and every tongue shall confess to God.

12. So then every one of us shall give account of himself to God.

13. Let us not therefore judge one another any more: but judge this rather, that no man put a stumblingblock or an occasion to fall in *his* brother's way.

14. I know, and am persuaded by the Lord Jesus, that *there is* nothing unclean of itself: but to him that esteemeth any thing to be unclean, to him *it is* unclean.

15. But if thy brother be grieved with *thy* meat, now walkest thou not charitably. Destroy not him with thy meat, for whom Christ died.

16. Let not then your good be evil spoken of:

17. For the kingdom of God is not meat and drink; but righteousness, and peace, and joy in the Holy Ghost.

18. For he that in these things serveth Christ *is* acceptable to God, and approved of men.

19. Let us therefore follow after the things which make for peace, and things wherewith one may edify another.

20. For meat destroy not the work of God. All things indeed *are* pure; but *it is* evil for that man who eateth with offense.

21. *It is* good neither to eat flesh, nor to drink wine, nor *any thing* whereby thy brother stumbleth, or is offended, or is made weak.

22. Hast thou faith? have *it* to thyself before God. Happy *is* he that condemneth not himself in that thing which he alloweth.

23. And he that doubteth is damned if he eat, because *he eateth* not of faith: for whatsoever *is* not of faith is sin.

CHAPTER FIFTEEN

We then that are strong ought to bear the infirmities of the weak, and not to please ourselves.

2. Let every one of us please *his* neighbor for *his* good to edification.

3. For even Christ pleased not himself; but, as it is written, The reproaches of them that reproached thee fell on me.

4. For whatsoever things were written aforetime were written for our learning, that we through patience and comfort of the Scriptures might have hope.

5. Now the God of patience and consolation grant you to be likeminded one toward another according to Christ Jesus:

6. That ye may with one mind *and* one mouth glorify God, even the Father of our Lord Jesus Christ.

7. Wherefore receive ye one another, as Christ also received us, to the glory of God.

8. Now I say that Jesus Christ was a minister of the circumcision for the truth of God, to confirm the promises *made* unto the fathers:

9. And that the Gĕn'tīleṣ might glorify God for *his* mercy; as it is written, For this cause I will confess to thee among the Gĕn'tīleṣ, and sing unto thy name.

10. And again he saith, Rejoice, ye Gĕn'tīleṣ, with his people.

11. And again, Praise the Lord, all ye Gĕn'tīleṣ; and laud him, all ye people.

12. And again, Ē-ṣā'ĭăs saith, There shall be a root of Jesse, and he that shall rise to reign over the Gĕn'tīleṣ; in him shall the Gĕn'tīleṣ trust.

13. Now the God of hope fill you with all joy and peace in believing, that ye may abound in hope, through the power of the Holy Ghost.

14. And I myself also am persuaded of you, my brethren, that ye also are full of goodness, filled with all knowledge, able also to admonish one another.

15. Nevertheless, brethren, I have written the more boldly unto you in some sort, as putting you in mind, because of the grace that is given to me of God,

16. That I should be the minister of Jesus Christ to the Gĕn'tīles̗, ministering the gospel of God, that the offering up of the Gĕn'tīles̗ might be acceptable, being sanctified by the Holy Ghost.

17. I have therefore whereof I may glory through Jesus Christ in those things which pertain to God.

18. For I will not dare to speak of any of those things which Christ hath not wrought by me, to make the Gĕn'tīles̗ obedient, by word and deed,

19. Through mighty signs and wonders, by the power of the Spirit of God; so that from Jerusalem, and round about unto Il-lўr'ĭ-cŭm, I have fully preached the gospel of Christ.

20. Yea, so have I strived to preach the gospel, not where Christ was named, lest I should build upon another man's foundation:

21. But as it is written, To whom he was not spoken of, they shall see: and they that have not heard shall understand.

22. For which cause also I have been much hindered from coming to you.

23. But now having no more place in these parts, and having a great desire these many years to come unto you;

24. Whensoever I take my journey into Spain, I will come to you: for I trust to see you in my journey, and to be brought on my way thitherward by you, if first I be somewhat filled with your *company*.

25. But now I go unto Jerusalem to minister unto the saints.

26. For it hath pleased them of Macedonia and Ȧ-ϵhā'i̯a to make a certain contribution for the poor saints which are at Jerusalem.

27. It hath pleased them verily; and their debtors they are. For if the Ğĕn'tīleṣ have been made partakers of their spiritual things, their duty is also to minister unto them in carnal things.

28. When therefore I have performed this, and have sealed to them this fruit, I will come by you into Spain.

29. And I am sure that, when I come unto you, I shall come in the fulness of the blessing of the gospel of Christ.

30. Now I beseech you, brethren, for the Lord Jesus Christ's sake, and for the love of the Spirit, that ye strive together with me in *your* prayers to God for me;

31. That I may be delivered from them that do not believe in Judea; and that my service which *I have* for Jerusalem may be accepted of the saints;

32. That I may come unto you with joy by the will of God, and may with you be refreshed.

33. Now the God of peace *be* with you all. Amen.

CHAPTER SIXTEEN

I commend unto you Phē'bē our sister, which is a servant of the church which is at Çĕn-ehrē'à:

2. That ye receive her in the Lord, as becometh saints, and that ye assist her in whatsoever business she hath need of you: for she hath been a succorer of many, and of myself also.

3. Greet Priscilla and Ăq'uĭ-là, my helpers in Christ Jesus:

4. Who have for my life laid down their own necks: unto whom not only I give thanks, but also all the churches of the Gĕn'tīleş.

5. Likewise *greet* the church that is in their house. Salute my well-beloved Ē-pē'nē-tŭs, who is the firstfruits of À-ehā'ịà unto Christ.

6. Greet Mary, who bestowed much labor on us.

7. Salute Ăn'drō-nī'cŭs and Jṵ'nĭ-à, my kinsmen, and my fellow prisoners, who are of note among the apostles, who also were in Christ before me.

8. Greet Ăm'plĭ-ăs, my beloved in the Lord.

9. Salute Ûr'bāne, our helper in Christ, and Stā'ϵhȳs my beloved.

10. Salute À-pĕl'lēṣ approved in Christ. Salute them which are of Ăr'ĭs-tō-bū'lŭs' *household.*

11. Salute Hē-rō'dĭ-ŏn my kinsman. Greet them that be of the *household* of Narcissus, which are in the Lord.

12. Salute Trȳ-phē'nà and Trȳ-phō'sà, who labor in the Lord. Salute the beloved Pēr'sĭs, which labored much in the Lord.

13. Salute Rufus chosen in the Lord, and his mother and mine.

14. Salute À-sȳn-crĭ-tŭs, Phlē'gŏn, Hēr'măs, Păt'rō-bàs, Hēr'mēṣ, and the brethren which are with them.

15. Salute Phī-lŏl'ō-gŭs, and Julia, Nē'reūs, and his sister, and Ō-lȳm'pĕs, and all the saints which are with them.

16. Salute one another with a holy kiss. The churches of Christ salute you.

17. Now I beseech you, brethren, mark them which cause divisions and offenses contrary to the doctrine which ye have learned; and avoid them.

18. For they that are such serve not our Lord Jesus Christ, but their own belly; and by good words and fair speeches deceive the hearts of the simple.

19. For your obedience is come abroad unto all *men*. I am glad therefore on your behalf: but yet I would have you wise unto that which is good, and simple concerning evil.

20. And the God of peace shall bruise Satan under your feet shortly. The grace of our Lord Jesus Christ *be* with you. Amen.

21. Tĭ-mō'thē-ŭs my workfellow, and Lucius, and Jā'sŏn, and Sō-sĭp'à-tēr, my kinsmen, salute you.

22. I Tēr'tĭ-ŭs, who wrote *this* epistle, salute you in the Lord.

23. Gā'iŭs mine host, and of the whole church, saluteth you. Ē-răs'tŭs the chamberlain of the city saluteth you, and Quartus a brother.

24. The grace of our Lord Jesus Christ *be* with you all. Amen.

25. Now to him that is of power to stablish you according to my gospel, and the preaching of Jesus Christ, according to the revelation of the mystery, which was kept secret since the world began,

26. But now is made manifest, and by the Scriptures of the prophets, according to the commandment of the everlasting God, made known to all nations for the obedience of faith:

27. To God only wise, *be* glory through Jesus Christ for ever. Amen.

PHILEMON

Paul, a prisoner of Jesus Christ, and Timothy *our* brother, unto Phĭ-lē'mŏn our dearly beloved, and fellow laborer.

2. And to *our* beloved Ăpph'ĭ-à, and Är-ᴄhĭp'pŭs our fellow soldier, and to the church in thy house:

3. Grace to you, and peace, from God our Father and the Lord Jesus Christ.

4. I thank my God, making mention of thee always in my prayers,

5. Hearing of thy love and faith, which thou hast toward the Lord Jesus, and toward all saints;

6. That the communication of thy faith may become effectual by the acknowledging of every good thing which is in you in Christ Jesus.

7. For we have great joy and consolation in thy love, because the bowels of the saints are refreshed by thee, brother.

8. Wherefore, though I might be much bold in Christ to enjoin thee that which is convenient,

9. Yet for love's sake I rather beseech *thee*, being such a one as Paul the aged, and now also a prisoner of Jesus Christ.

10. I beseech thee for my son Ŏ-nĕs'ĭ-mŭs, whom I have begotten in my bonds:

11. Which in time past was to thee unprofitable, but now profitable to thee and to me:

12. Whom I have sent again: thou therefore receive him, that is, mine own bowels:

13. Whom I would have retained with me, that in thy stead he might have ministered unto me in the bonds of the gospel:

14. But without thy mind would I do nothing; that thy benefit should not be as it were of necessity, but willingly.

15. For perhaps he therefore departed for a season, that thou shouldest receive him for ever;

16. Not now as a servant, but above a servant, a brother beloved, specially to me, but how much more unto thee, both in the flesh, and in the Lord?

17. If thou count me therefore a partner, receive him as myself.

18. If he hath wronged thee, or oweth *thee* aught, put that on mine account;

19. I Paul have written *it* with mine own hand, I will repay *it:* albeit I do not say to thee how thou owest unto me even thine own self besides.

20. Yea, brother, let me have joy of thee in the Lord: refresh my bowels in the Lord.

21. Having confidence in thy obedience I wrote unto thee, knowing that thou wilt also do more than I say.

22. But withal prepare me also a lodging: for I trust that through your prayers I shall be given unto you.

23. There salute thee Ĕp'à-phrăs, my fellow prisoner in Christ Jesus;

24. Marcus, Ăr'ĭs-tär'€hŭs, Dē'măs, Lū'càs, my fellow la-borers.

25. The grace of our Lord Jesus Christ *be* with your spirit. Amen.

PHILIPPIANS

CHAPTER ONE

Paul and Tĭ-mo'thē-ŭs, the servants of Jesus Christ, to all the saints in Christ Jesus which are at Phĭ-lĭp'pī, with the bishops and deacons:

2. Grace *be* unto you, and peace, from God our Father and *from* the Lord Jesus Christ.

3. I thank my God upon every remembrance of you,

4. Always in every prayer of mine for you all making request with joy,

5. For your fellowship in the gospel from the first day until now;

6. Being confident of this very thing, that he which hath begun a good work in you will perform *it* until the day of Jesus Christ:

7. Even as it is meet for me to think this of you all, because I have you in my heart; inasmuch as both in my bonds, and in the defense and confirmation of the gospel, ye all are partakers of my grace.

8. For God is my record, how greatly I long after you all in the bowels of Jesus Christ.

9. And this I pray, that your love may abound yet more and more in knowledge and *in* all judgment;

10. That ye may approve things that are excellent; that ye may be sincere and without offense till the day of Christ;

11. Being filled with the fruits of righteousness, which are by Jesus Christ, unto the glory and praise of God.

12. But I would ye should understand, brethren, that the things *which happened* unto me have fallen out rather unto the furtherance of the gospel;

13. So that my bonds in Christ are manifest in all the palace, and in all other *places;*

14. And many of the brethren in the Lord, waxing confident by my bonds, are much more bold to speak the word without fear.

15. Some indeed preach Christ even of envy and strife; and some also of good will:

16. The one preach Christ of contention, not sincerely, supposing to add affliction to my bonds:

17. But the other of love, knowing that I am set for the defense of the gospel.

18. What then? notwithstanding, every way, whether in pretense, or in truth, Christ is preached; and I therein do rejoice, yea, and will rejoice.

19. For I know that this shall turn to my salvation through your prayer, and the supply of the Spirit of Jesus Christ,

20. According to my earnest expectation and *my* hope, that in nothing I shall be ashamed, but *that* with all boldness, as always, *so* now also Christ shall be magnified in my body, whether *it be* by life, or by death.

21. For to me to live *is* Christ, and to die *is* gain.

22. But if I live in the flesh, this *is* the fruit of my labor: yet what I shall choose I wot not.

23. For I am in a strait betwixt two, having a desire to depart, and to be with Christ; which is far better:

24. Nevertheless to abide in the flesh *is* more needful for you.

25. And having this confidence, I know that I shall abide and continue with you all for your furtherance and joy of faith;

26. That your rejoicing may be more abundant in Jesus Christ for me by my coming to you again.

27. Only let your conversation be as it becometh the gospel of Christ: that whether I come and see you, or else be absent,

I may hear of your affairs, that ye stand fast in one spirit, with one mind striving together for the faith of the gospel;

28. And in nothing terrified by your adversaries: which is to them an evident token of perdition, but to you of salvation, and that of God.

29. For unto you it is given in the behalf of Christ, not only to believe on him, but also to suffer for his sake;

30. Having the same conflict which ye saw in me, and now hear *to be* in me.

CHAPTER TWO

If *there be* therefore any consolation in Christ, if any comfort of love, if any fellowship of the Spirit, if any bowels and mercies,

2. Fulfil ye my joy, that ye be likeminded, having the same love, *being* of one accord, of one mind.

3. *Let* nothing *be done* through strife or vainglory; but in lowliness of mind let each esteem other better than themselves.

4. Look not every man on his own things, but every man also on the things of others.

PHILIPPIANS

5. Let this mind be in you, which was also in Christ Jesus:

6. Who, being in the form of God, thought it not robbery to be equal with God:

7. But made himself of no reputation, and took upon him the form of a servant, and was made in the likeness of men:

8. And being found in fashion as a man, he humbled himself, and became obedient unto death, even the death of the cross.

9. Wherefore God also hath highly exalted him, and given him a name which is above every name:

10. That at the name of Jesus every knee should bow, of *things* in heaven, and *things* in earth, and *things* under the earth;

11. And *that* every tongue should confess that Jesus Christ *is* Lord, to the glory of God the Father.

12. Wherefore, my beloved, as ye have always obeyed, not as in my presence only, but now much more in my absence, work out your own salvation with fear and trembling:

13. For it is God which worketh in you both to will and to do of *his* good pleasure.

14. Do all things without murmurings and disputings:

15. That ye may be blameless and harmless, the sons of God, without rebuke, in the midst of a crooked and perverse nation, among whom ye shine as lights in the world;

16. Holding forth the word of life; that I may rejoice in the day of Christ, that I have not run in vain, neither labored in vain.

17. Yea, and if I be offered upon the sacrifice and service of your faith, I joy, and rejoice with you all.

18. For the same cause also do ye joy, and rejoice with me.

19. But I trust in the Lord Jesus to send Tĭ-mō'thē-ŭs shortly unto you, that I also may be of good comfort, when I know your state.

20. For I have no man likeminded, who will naturally care for your state.

21. For all seek their own, not the things which are Jesus Christ's.

22. But ye know the proof of him, that, as a son with the father, he hath served with me in the gospel.

23. Him therefore I hope to send presently, so soon as I shall see how it will go with me.

24. But I trust in the Lord that I also myself shall come shortly.

25. Yet I supposed it necessary to send to you Ē-păph'rō-dī'tūs, my brother, and companion in labor, and fellow soldier, but your messenger, and he that ministered to my wants.

26. For he longed after you all, and was full of heaviness, because that ye had heard that he had been sick.

27. For indeed he was sick nigh unto death: but God had mercy on him; and not on him only, but on me also, lest I should have sorrow upon sorrow.

28. I sent him therefore the more carefully, that, when ye see him again, ye may rejoice, and that I may be the less sorrowful.

29. Receive him therefore in the Lord with all gladness; and hold such in reputation:

30. Because for the work of Christ he was nigh unto death, not regarding his life, to supply your lack of service toward me.

CHAPTER THREE

Finally, my brethren, rejoice in the Lord. To write the same things to you, to me indeed *is* not grievous, but for you *it is* safe.

2. Beware of dogs, beware of evil workers, beware of the concision.

3. For we are the circumcision, which worship God in the spirit, and rejoice in Christ Jesus, and have no confidence in the flesh.

4. Though I might also have confidence in the flesh. If any other man thinketh that he hath whereof he might trust in the flesh, I more:

5. Circumcised the eighth day, of the stock of Ĭṣ'rā-ĕl, *of* the tribe of Benjamin, a Hebrew of the Hebrews; as touching the law, a Phăr'ĭ-sēe;

6. Concerning zeal, persecuting the church; touching the righteousness which is in the law, blameless.

7. But what things were gain to me, those I counted loss for Christ.

8. Yea doubtless, and I count all things *but* loss for the excellency of the knowledge of Christ Jesus my Lord: for whom I have suffered the loss of all things, and do count them *but* dung, that I may win Christ,

9. And be found in him, not having mine own righteousness, which is of the law, but that which is through the faith of Christ, the righteousness which is of God by faith:

10. That I may know him, and the power of his resurrection, and the fellowship of his sufferings, being made conformable unto his death;

11. If by any means I might attain unto the resurrection of the dead.

12. Not as though I had already attained, either were already perfect: but I follow after, if that I may apprehend that for which also I am apprehended of Christ Jesus.

13. Brethren, I count not myself to have apprehended: but *this* one thing *I do*, forgetting those things which are behind, and reaching forth unto those things which are before,

14. I press toward the mark for the prize of the high calling of God in Christ Jesus.

15. Let us therefore, as many as be perfect, be thus minded: and if in any thing ye be otherwise minded, God shall reveal even this unto you.

16. Nevertheless, whereto we have already attained, let us walk by the same rule, let us mind the same thing.

17. Brethren, be followers together of me, and mark them which walk so as ye have us for an ensample.

18. (For many walk, of whom I have told you often, and now tell you even weeping, *that they are* the enemies of the cross of Christ:

19. Whose end *is* destruction, whose God *is their* belly, and *whose* glory *is* in their shame, who mind earthly things.)

20. For our conversation is in heaven; from whence also we look for the Saviour, the Lord Jesus Christ:

21. Who shall change our vile body, that it may be fashioned like unto his glorious body, according to the working whereby he is able even to subdue all things unto himself.

CHAPTER FOUR

Therefore, my brethren dearly beloved and longed for, my joy and crown, so stand fast in the Lord, *my* dearly beloved.

2. I beseech Eū-ō'dĭ-ăs, and beseech Sy̆n'ty̆-ehē, that they be of the same mind in the Lord.

3. And I entreat thee also, true yokefellow, help those women which labored with me in the gospel, with Clement also, and *with* other my fellow laborers, whose names *are* in the book of life.

4. Rejoice in the Lord always: *and* again I say, Rejoice.

5. Let your moderation be known unto all men. The Lord *is* at hand.

6. Be careful for nothing; but in every thing by prayer and supplication with thanksgiving let your requests be made known unto God.

7. And the peace of God, which passeth all understanding, shall keep your hearts and minds through Christ Jesus.

8. Finally, brethren, whatsoever things are true, whatsoever things *are* honest, whatsoever things *are* just, whatsoever things *are* pure, whatsoever things *are* lovely, whatsoever things *are* of good report; if *there be* any virtue, and if *there be* any praise, think on these things.

9. Those things, which ye have both learned, and received, and heard, and seen in me, do: and the God of peace shall be with you.

10. But I rejoiced in the Lord greatly, that now at the last your care of me hath flourished again; wherein ye were also careful, but ye lacked opportunity.

11. Not that I speak in respect of want: for I have learned, in whatsoever state I am, *therewith* to be content.

12. I know both how to be abased, and I know how to abound: every where and in all things I am instructed both to be full and to be hungry, both to abound and to suffer need.

13. I can do all things through Christ which strengtheneth me.

14. Notwithstanding, ye have well done, that ye did communicate with my affliction.

15. Now ye Phĭ-lĭp'pĭ-ănṣ know also, that in the beginning of the gospel, when I departed from Macedonia, no church communicated with me as concerning giving and receiving, but ye only.

16. For even in Thĕs'sà-lō-nī'cà ye sent once and again unto my necessity.

17. Not because I desire a gift: but I desire fruit that may abound to your account.

18. But I have all, and abound: I am full, having received of Ē-păph'rō-dī'tŭs the things *which were sent* from you, an odor of a sweet smell, a sacrifice acceptable, well-pleasing to God.

19. But my God shall supply all your need according to his riches in glory by Christ Jesus.

20. Now unto God and our Father *be* glory for ever and ever. Amen.

21. Salute every saint in Christ Jesus. The brethren which are with me greet you.

22. All the saints salute you, chiefly they that are of Cæsar's household.

23. The grace of our Lord Jesus Christ *be* with you all. Amen.

The Pauline authorship of the following works is problematic at best and widely disputed or rejected at worst. In the case of the Epistle to the Hebrews, Pauline authorship is universally denied.

COLOSSIANS

CHAPTER ONE

Paul, an apostle of Jesus Christ by the will of God, and Tĭ-mō'thē-ŭs *our* brother,

2. To the saints and faithful brethren in Christ which are at Cō-lŏs'sē: Grace *be* unto you, and peace, from God our Father and the Lord Jesus Christ.

3. We give thanks to God and the Father of our Lord Jesus Christ, praying always for you,

4. Since we heard of your faith in Christ Jesus, and of the love *which ye have* to all the saints,

5. For the hope which is laid up for you in heaven, whereof ye heard before in the word of the truth of the gospel;

6. Which is come unto you, as *it is* in all the world; and bringeth forth fruit, as *it doth* also in you, since the day ye heard *of it*, and knew the grace of God in truth:

7. As ye also learned of Ĕp'à-phrăs our dear fellow servant, who is for you a faithful minister of Christ;

8. Who also declared unto us your love in the Spirit.

9. For this cause we also, since the day we heard *it*, do not cease to pray for you, and to desire that ye might be filled with the knowledge of his will in all wisdom and spiritual understanding;

10. That ye might walk worthy of the Lord unto all pleasing, being fruitful in every good work, and increasing in the knowledge of God;

11. Strengthened with all might, according to his glorious power, unto all patience and long-suffering with joyfulness;

12. Giving thanks unto the Father, which hath made us meet to be partakers of the inheritance of the saints in light:

13. Who hath delivered us from the power of darkness, and hath translated *us* into the kingdom of his dear Son:

14. In whom we have redemption through his blood, *even* the forgiveness of sins:

15. Who is the image of the invisible God, the firstborn of every creature:

16. For by him were all things created, that are in heaven, and that are in earth, visible and invisible, whether *they be* thrones, or dominions, or principalities, or powers: all things were created by him, and for him:

17. And he is before all things, and by him all things consist:

18. And he is the head of the body, the church: who is the beginning, the firstborn from the dead; that in all things he might have the preeminence.

19. For it pleased *the Father* that in him should all fulness dwell;

20. And, having made peace through the blood of his cross, by him to reconcile all things unto himself; by him, *I say*, whether *they be* things in earth, or things in heaven.

21. And you, that were sometime alienated and enemies in *your* mind by wicked works, yet now hath he reconciled

22. In the body of his flesh through death, to present you holy and unblamable and unreprovable in his sight:

23. If ye continue in the faith grounded and settled, and *be* not moved away from the hope of the gospel, which ye have heard, *and* which was preached to every creature which is under heaven; whereof I Paul am made a minister;

24. Who now rejoice in my sufferings for you, and fill up that which is behind of the afflictions of Christ in my flesh for his body's sake, which is the church:

25. Whereof I am made a minister, according to the dispensation of God which is given to me for you, to fulfil the word of God;

26. *Even* the mystery which hath been hid from ages and from generations, but now is made manifest to his saints:

27. To whom God would make known what *is* the riches of the glory of this mystery among the Gĕn'tīleṣ; which is Christ in you, the hope of glory:

28. Whom we preach, warning every man, and teaching every man in all wisdom; that we may present every man perfect in Christ Jesus:

29. Whereunto I also labor, striving according to his working, which worketh in me mightily.

CHAPTER TWO

For I would that ye knew what great conflict I have for you, and *for* them at Lā-ŏd'ĭ-çē'à, and *for* as many as have not seen my face in the flesh;

2. That their hearts might be comforted, being knit together in love, and unto all riches of the full assurance of understanding, to the acknowledgment of the mystery of God, and of the Father, and of Christ;

3. In whom are hid all the treasures of wisdom and knowledge.

4. And this I say, lest any man should beguile you with enticing words.

5. For though I be absent in the flesh, yet am I with you in the spirit, joying and beholding your order, and the steadfastness of your faith in Christ.

6. As ye have therefore received Christ Jesus the Lord, *so* walk ye in him:

7. Rooted and built up in him, and stablished in the faith, as ye have been taught, abounding therein with thanksgiving.

8. Beware lest any man spoil you through philosophy and vain deceit, after the tradition of men, after the rudiments of the world, and not after Christ.

9. For in him dwelleth all the fulness of the Godhead bodily.

10. And ye are complete in him, which is the head of all principality and power:

11. In whom also ye are circumcised with the circumcision made without hands, in putting off the body of the sins of the flesh by the circumcision of Christ:

12. Buried with him in baptism, wherein also ye are risen with *him* through the faith of the operation of God, who hath raised him from the dead.

13. And you, being dead in your sins and the uncircumcision of your flesh, hath he quickened together with him, having forgiven you all trespasses;

14. Blotting out the handwriting of ordinances that was against us, which was contrary to us, and took it out of the way, nailing it to his cross;

15. *And* having spoiled principalities and powers, he made a show of them openly, triumphing over them in it.

16. Let no man therefore judge you in meat, or in drink, or in respect of a holyday, or of the new moon, or of the sabbath *days:*

17. Which are a shadow of things to come; but the body *is* of Christ.

18. Let no man beguile you of your reward in a voluntary humility and worshipping of angels, intruding into those things which he hath not seen, vainly puffed up by his fleshly mind,

19. And not holding the Head, from which all the body by joints and bands having nourishment ministered, and knit together, increaseth with the increase of God.

20. Wherefore if ye be dead with Christ from the rudiments of the world, why, as though living in the world, are ye subject to ordinances,

21. (Touch not; taste not; handle not;

22. Which all are to perish with the using;) after the commandments and doctrines of men?

23. Which things have indeed a show of wisdom in will-worship, and humility, and neglecting of the body; not in any honor to the satisfying of the flesh.

CHAPTER THREE

If ye then be risen with Christ, seek those things which are above, where Christ sitteth on the right hand of God.

2. Set your affection on things above, not on things on the earth.

3. For ye are dead, and your life is hid with Christ in God.

4. When Christ, *who is* our life, shall appear, then shall ye also appear with him in glory.

5. Mortify therefore your members which are upon the earth; fornication, uncleanness, inordinate affection, evil concupiscence, and covetousness, which is idolatry:

6. For which things' sake the wrath of God cometh on the children of disobedience:

7. In the which ye also walked sometime, when ye lived in them.

8. But now ye also put off all these; anger, wrath, malice, blasphemy, filthy communication out of your mouth.

9. Lie not one to another, seeing that ye have put off the old man with his deeds;

10. And have put on the new *man*, which is renewed in knowledge after the image of him that created him:

11. Where there is neither Greek nor Jew, circumcision nor uncircumcision, Barbarian, Scÿth'ĭ-ăn, bond *nor* free: but Christ *is* all, and in all.

12. Put on therefore, as the elect of God, holy and beloved, bowels of mercies, kindness, humbleness of mind, meekness, long-suffering;

13. Forbearing one another, and forgiving one another, if any man have a quarrel against any: even as Christ forgave you, so also *do* ye.

14. And above all these things *put on* charity, which is the bond of perfectness.

15. And let the peace of God rule in your hearts, to the which also ye are called in one body; and be ye thankful.

16. Let the word of Christ dwell in you richly in all wisdom; teaching and admonishing one another in psalms and hymns and spiritual songs, singing with grace in your hearts to the Lord.

17. And whatsoever ye do in word or deed, *do* all in the name of the Lord Jesus, giving thanks to God and the Father by him.

18. Wives, submit yourselves unto your own husbands, as it is fit in the Lord.

19. Husbands, love *your* wives, and be not bitter against them.

20. Children, obey *your* parents in all things: for this is well-pleasing unto the Lord.

21. Fathers, provoke not your children *to anger*, lest they be discouraged.

22. Servants, obey in all things *your* masters according to the flesh; not with eyeservice, as menpleasers; but in singleness of heart, fearing God:

23. And whatsoever ye do, do *it* heartily, as to the Lord, and not unto men;

24. Knowing that of the Lord ye shall receive the reward of the inheritance: for ye serve the Lord Christ.

25. But he that doeth wrong shall receive for the wrong which he hath done: and there is no respect of persons.

CHAPTER FOUR

Masters, give unto *your* servants that which is just and equal; knowing that ye also have a Master in heaven.

2. Continue in prayer, and watch in the same with thanksgiving;

3. Withal praying also for us, that God would open unto us a door of utterance, to speak the mystery of Christ, for which I am also in bonds:

4. That I may make it manifest, as I ought to speak.

5. Walk in wisdom toward them that are without, redeeming the time.

6. Let your speech *be* always with grace, seasoned with salt, that ye may know how ye ought to answer every man.

7. All my state shall Tўєh'ĭ-cŭs declare unto you, *who is* a beloved brother, and a faithful minister and fellow servant in the Lord:

8. Whom I have sent unto you for the same purpose, that he might know your estate, and comfort your hearts;

9. With Ō-nĕs'ĭ-mŭs, a faithful and beloved brother, who is *one* of you. They shall make known unto you all things which *are done* here.

10. Ăr'ĭs-tär'ҽhŭs my fellow prisoner saluteth you, and Marcus, sister's son to Barnabas, (touching whom ye received commandments: if he come unto you, receive him;)

11. And Jesus, which is called Justus, who are of the circumcision. These only *are my* fellow workers unto the kingdom of God, which have been a comfort unto me.

12. Ĕp'à-phrăs, who is *one* of you, a servant of Christ, saluteth you, always laboring fervently for you in prayers, that ye may stand perfect and complete in all the will of God.

13. For I bear him record, that he hath a great zeal for you, and them *that are* in Lā-ŏd'ĭ-çē'à, and them in Hī'ĕr-ăp'ō-lĭs.

14. Luke, the beloved physician, and Dē'măs, greet you.

15. Salute the brethren which are in Lā-ŏd'ĭ-çā'à, and Nўm'phăs, and the church which is in his house.

16. And when this epistle is read among you, cause that it be read also in the church of the Lā-ŏd'ĭ-cē'ănṣ; and that ye likewise read the *epistle* from Lā-ŏd'ĭ-cē'à.

17. And say to Är-ehĭp'pŭs, Take heed to the ministry which thou hast received in the Lord, that thou fulfil it.

18. The salutation by the hand of me Paul. Remember my bonds. Grace *be* with you. Amen.

EPHESIANS

CHAPTER ONE

Paul, an apostle of Jesus Christ by the will of God, to the saints which are at Ĕph'ĕ-sŭs, and to the faithful in Christ Jesus:

2. Grace *be* to you, and peace, from God our Father, and *from* the Lord Jesus Christ.

3. Blessed *be* the God and Father of our Lord Jesus Christ, who hath blessed us with all spiritual blessings in heavenly *places* in Christ:

4. According as he hath chosen us in him before the foundation of the world, that we should be holy and without blame before him in love:

5. Having predestinated us unto the adoption of children by Jesus Christ to himself, according to the good pleasure of his will,

6. To the praise of the glory of his grace, wherein he hath made us accepted in the beloved:

7. In whom we have redemption through his blood, the forgiveness of sins, according to the riches of his grace;

8. Wherein he hath abounded toward us in all wisdom and prudence;

9. Having made known unto us the mystery of his will, according to his good pleasure which he hath purposed in himself:

10. That in the dispensation of the fulness of times he might gather together in one all things in Christ, both which are in heaven, and which are on earth; *even* in him:

11. In whom also we have obtained an inheritance, being predestinated according to the purpose of him who worketh all things after the counsel of his own will:

12. That we should be to the praise of his glory, who first trusted in Christ.

13. In whom ye also *trusted*, after that ye heard the word of truth, the gospel of your salvation: in whom also, after that ye believed, ye were sealed with that Holy Spirit of promise,

14. Which is the earnest of our inheritance until the redemption of the purchased possession, unto the praise of his glory.

15. Wherefore I also, after I heard of your faith in the Lord Jesus, and love unto all the saints,

16. Cease not to give thanks for you, making mention of you in my prayers;

17. That the God of our Lord Jesus Christ, the Father of glory, may give unto you the spirit of wisdom and revelation in the knowledge of him:

18. The eyes of your understanding being enlightened; that ye may know what is the hope of his calling, and what the riches of the glory of his inheritance in the saints,

19. And what *is* the exceeding greatness of his power to us-ward who believe, according to the working of his mighty power,

20. Which he wrought in Christ, when he raised him from the dead, and set *him* at his own right hand in the heavenly *places*,

21. Far above all principality, and power, and might, and dominion, and every name that is named, not only in this world, but also in that which is to come:

22. And hath put all *things* under his feet, and gave him *to be* the head over all *things* to the church,

23. Which is his body, the fulness of him that filleth all in all.

CHAPTER TWO

And you *hath he quickened*, who were dead in trespasses and sins;

2. Wherein in time past ye walked according to the course of this world, according to the prince of the power of the air, the spirit that now worketh in the children of disobedience:

3. Among whom also we all had our conversation in times past in the lusts of our flesh, fulfilling the desires of the flesh and of the mind; and were by nature the children of wrath, even as others.

4. But God, who is rich in mercy, for his great love wherewith he loved us,

5. Even when we were dead in sins, hath quickened us together with Christ, (by grace ye are saved;)

6. And hath raised *us* up together, and made *us* sit together in heavenly *places* in Christ Jesus:

7. That in the ages to come he might show the exceeding riches of his grace, in *his* kindness toward us, through Christ Jesus.

8. For by grace are ye saved through faith; and that not of yourselves: *it is* the gift of God:

9. Not of works, lest any man should boast.

10. For we are his workmanship, created in Christ Jesus unto good works, which God hath before ordained that we should walk in them.

11. Wherefore remember, that ye *being* in time past Gĕn'tīleṣ in the flesh, who are called Uncircumcision by that which is called the Circumcision in the flesh made by hands;

12. That at that time ye were without Christ, being aliens from the commonwealth of Ĭṣ'rā-ĕl, and strangers from the covenants of promise, having no hope, and without God in the world:

13. But now, in Christ Jesus, ye who sometime were far off are made nigh by the blood of Christ.

14. For he is our peace, who hath made both one, and hath broken down the middle wall of partition *between us*;

15. Having abolished in his flesh the enmity, *even* the law of commandments *contained* in ordinances; for to make in himself of twain one new man, *so* making peace;

16. And that he might reconcile both unto God in one body by the cross, having slain the enmity thereby:

17. And came and preached peace to you which were afar off, and to them that were nigh.

18. For through him we both have access by one Spirit unto the Father.

19. Now therefore ye are no more strangers and foreigners, but fellow citizens with the saints, and of the household of God;

20. And are built upon the foundation of the apostles and prophets, Jesus Christ himself being the chief corner *stone*;

21. In whom all the building fitly framed together groweth unto a holy temple in the Lord:

22. In whom ye also are builded together for a habitation of God through the Spirit.

CHAPTER THREE

For this cause I Paul, the prisoner of Jesus Christ for you Gĕn'tīleṣ,

2. If ye have heard of the dispensation of the grace of God which is given me to you-ward:

3. How that by revelation he made known unto me the mystery; (as I wrote afore in few words;

4. Whereby, when ye read, ye may understand my knowledge in the mystery of Christ,)

5. Which in other ages was not made known unto the sons of men, as it is now revealed unto his holy apostles and prophets by the Spirit;

6. That the Gĕn'tīleṣ should be fellow heirs, and of the same body, and partakers of his promise in Christ by the gospel:

7. Whereof I was made a minister, according to the gift of the grace of God given unto me by the effectual working of his power.

8. Unto me, who am less than the least of all saints, is this grace given, that I should preach among the Gĕn'tīleṣ the unsearchable riches of Christ;

9. And to make all *men* see what *is* the fellowship of the mystery, which from the beginning of the world hath been hid in God, who created all things by Jesus Christ:

10. To the intent that now unto the principalities and powers in heavenly *places* might be known by the church the manifold wisdom of God,

11. According to the eternal purpose which he purposed in Christ Jesus our Lord:

12. In whom we have boldness and access with confidence by the faith of him.

13. Wherefore I desire that ye faint not at my tribulations for you, which is your glory.

14. For this cause I bow my knees unto the Father of our Lord Jesus Christ,

15. Of whom the whole family in heaven and earth is named,

16. That he would grant you, according to the riches of his glory, to be strengthened with might by his Spirit in the inner man;

17. That Christ may dwell in your hearts by faith; that ye, being rooted and grounded in love,

18. May be able to comprehend with all saints what *is* the breadth, and length, and depth, and height;

19. And to know the love of Christ, which passeth knowledge, that ye might be filled with all the fulness of God.

20. Now unto him that is able to do exceeding abundantly above all that we ask or think, according to the power that worketh in us,

21. Unto him *be* glory in the church by Christ Jesus throughout all ages, world without end. Amen.

CHAPTER FOUR

I therefore, the prisoner of the Lord, beseech you that ye walk worthy of the vocation wherewith ye are called,

2. With all lowliness and meekness, with long-suffering, forbearing one another in love;

3. Endeavoring to keep the unity of the Spirit in the bond of peace.

4. *There is* one body, and one Spirit, even as ye are called in one hope of your calling;

5. One Lord, one faith, one baptism,

6. One God and Father of all, who *is* above all, and through all, and in you all.

7. But unto every one of us is given grace according to the measure of the gift of Christ.

8. Wherefore he saith, When he ascended up on high, he led captivity captive, and gave gifts unto men.

9. (Now that he ascended, what is it but that he also descended first into the lower parts of the earth?

10. He that descended is the same also that ascended up far above all heavens, that he might fill all things.)

11. And he gave some, apostles; and some, prophets; and some, evangelists; and some, pastors and teachers;

12. For the perfecting of the saints, for the work of the ministry, for the edifying of the body of Christ:

13. Till we all come in the unity of the faith, and of the knowledge of the Son of God, unto a perfect man, unto the measure of the stature of the fulness of Christ:

14. That we *henceforth* be no more children, tossed to and fro, and carried about with every wind of doctrine, by the sleight of men, *and* cunning craftiness whereby they lie in wait to deceive;

15. But speaking the truth in love, may grow up into him in all things, which is the head, *even* Christ:

16. From whom the whole body fitly joined together and compacted by that which every joint supplieth, according to the effectual working in the measure of every part, maketh increase of the body unto the edifying of itself in love.

17. This I say therefore, and testify in the Lord, that ye henceforth walk not as other Gĕn'tīleṣ walk, in the vanity of their mind,

18. Having the understanding darkened, being alienated from the life of God through the ignorance that is in them, because of the blindness of their heart:

19. Who being past feeling have given themselves over unto lasciviousness, to work all uncleanness with greediness.

20. But ye have not so learned Christ;

21. If so be that ye have heard him, and have been taught by him, as the truth is in Jesus:

22. That ye put off concerning the former conversation the old man, which is corrupt according to the deceitful lusts;

23. And be renewed in the spirit of your mind;

24. And that ye put on the new man, which after God is created in righteousness and true holiness.

25. Wherefore putting away lying, speak every man truth with his neighbor: for we are members one of another.

26. Be ye angry, and sin not: let not the sun go down upon your wrath:

27. Neither give place to the devil.

28. Let him that stole steal no more: but rather let him labor, working with *his* hands the thing which is good, that he may have to give to him that needeth.

29. Let no corrupt communication proceed out of your mouth, but that which is good to the use of edifying, that it may minister grace unto the hearers.

30. And grieve not the Holy Spirit of God, whereby ye are sealed unto the day of redemption.

31. Let all bitterness, and wrath, and anger, and clamor, and evil speaking, be put away from you, with all malice:

32. And be ye kind one to another, tender-hearted, forgiving one another, even as God for Christ's sake hath forgiven you.

CHAPTER FIVE

Be ye therefore followers of God, as dear children;

2. And walk in love, as Christ also hath loved us, and hath given himself for us an offering and a sacrifice to God for a sweetsmelling savor.

3. But fornication, and all uncleanness, or covetousness, let it not be once named among you, as becometh saints;

4. Neither filthiness, nor foolish talking, nor jesting, which are not convenient: but rather giving of thanks.

5. For this ye know, that no whoremonger, nor unclean person, nor covetous man, who is an idolater, hath any inheritance in the kingdom of Christ and of God.

6. Let no man deceive you with vain words: for because of these things cometh the wrath of God upon the children of disobedience.

7. Be not ye therefore partakers with them.

8. For ye were sometime darkness, but now *are ye* light in the Lord: walk as children of light;

9. (For the fruit of the Spirit *is* in all goodness and righteousness and truth;)

10. Proving what is acceptable unto the Lord.

11. And have no fellowship with the unfruitful works of darkness, but rather reprove *them*.

12. For it is a shame even to speak of those things which are done of them in secret.

13. But all things that are reproved are made manifest by the light: for whatsoever doth make manifest is light.

14. Wherefore he saith, Awake thou that sleepest, and arise from the dead, and Christ shall give thee light.

15. See then that ye walk circumspectly, not as fools, but as wise,

16. Redeeming the time, because the days are evil.

17. Wherefore be ye not unwise, but understanding what the will of the Lord *is*.

18. And be not drunk with wine, wherein is excess; but be filled with the Spirit;

19. Speaking to yourselves in psalms and hymns and spiritual songs, singing and making melody in your heart to the Lord;

20. Giving thanks always for all things unto God and the Father in the name of our Lord Jesus Christ;

21. Submitting yourselves one to another in the fear of God.

22. Wives, submit yourselves unto your husband, as unto the Lord.

23. For the husband is the head of the wife, even as Christ is the head of the church: and he is the saviour of the body.

24. Therefore as the church is subject unto Christ, so *let* the wives *be* to their own husbands in every thing.

25. Husbands, love your wives, even as Christ also loved the church, and gave himself for it;

26. That he might sanctify and cleanse it with the washing of water by the word,

27. That he might present it to himself a glorious church, not having spot, or wrinkle, or any such thing; but that it should be holy and without blemish.

28. So ought men to love their wives as their own bodies. He that loveth his wife loveth himself.

29. For no man ever yet hated his own flesh; but nourisheth and cherisheth it, even as the Lord the church:

30. For we are members of his body, of his flesh, and of his bones.

31. For this cause shall a man leave his father and mother, and shall be joined unto his wife, and they two shall be one flesh.

32. This is a great mystery: but I speak concerning Christ and the church.

33. Nevertheless, let every one of you in particular so love his wife even as himself; and the wife *see* that she reverence *her* husband.

CHAPTER SIX

Children, obey your parents in the Lord: for this is right.

2. Honor thy father and mother; which is the first commandment with promise;

3. That it may be well with thee, and thou mayest live long on the earth.

4. And, ye fathers, provoke not your children to wrath: but bring them up in the nurture and admonition of the Lord.

5. Servants, be obedient to them that are *your* masters according to the flesh, with fear and trembling, in singleness of your heart, as unto Christ;

6. Not with eyeservice, as menpleasers; but as the servants of Christ, doing the will of God from the heart;

7. With good will doing service, as to the Lord, and not to men:

8. Knowing that whatsoever good thing any man doeth, the same shall he receive of the Lord, whether *he be* bond or free.

9. And, ye masters, do the same things unto them, forbearing threatening: knowing that your Master also is in heaven; neither is there respect of persons with him.

10. Finally, my brethren, be strong in the Lord, and in the power of his might.

11. Put on the whole armor of God, that ye may be able to stand against the wiles of the devil.

12. For we wrestle not against flesh and blood, but against principalities, against powers, against the rulers of the darkness of this world, against spiritual wickedness in high *places.*

13. Wherefore take unto you the whole armor of God, that ye may be able to withstand in the evil day, and having done all, to stand.

14. Stand therefore, having your loins girt about with truth, and having on the breastplate of righteousness;

15. And your feet shod with the preparation of the gospel of peace;

16. Above all, taking the shield of faith, wherewith ye shall be able to quench all the fiery darts of the wicked.

17. And take the helmet of salvation, and the sword of the Spirit, which is the word of God:

18. Praying always with all prayer and supplication in the Spirit, and watching thereunto with all perseverance and supplication for all saints;

19. And for me, that utterance may be given unto me, that I may open my mouth boldly, to make known the mystery of the gospel,

20. For which I am an ambassador in bonds; that therein I may speak boldly, as I ought to speak.

21. But that ye also may know my affairs, *and* how I do, Tўєh´ĭ-cŭs, a beloved brother and faithful minister in the Lord, shall make known to you all things:

22. Whom I have sent unto you for the same purpose, that ye might know our affairs, and *that* he might comfort your hearts.

23. Peace *be* to the brethren, and love with faith, from God the Father and the Lord Jesus Christ.

24. Grace *be* with all them that love our Lord Jesus Christ in sincerity. Amen.

1 TIMOTHY

CHAPTER ONE

Paul, an apostle of Jesus Christ by the commandment of God our Saviour, and Lord Jesus Christ, *which is* our hope;

2. Unto Timothy, *my* own son in the faith: Grace, mercy, *and* peace, from God our Father, and Jesus Christ our Lord.

3. As I besought thee to abide still at Ĕph'ē-sŭs, when I went into Macedonia, that thou mightest charge some that they teach no other doctrine,

4. Neither give heed to fables and endless genealogies, which minister questions, rather than godly edifying which is in faith: *so do.*

5. Now the end of the commandment is charity out of a pure heart, and *of* a good conscience, and *of* faith unfeigned:

6. From which some having swerved have turned aside unto vain jangling;

7. Desiring to be teachers of the law; understanding neither what they say, nor whereof they affirm.

8. But we know that the law *is* good, if a man use it lawfully;

9. Knowing this, that the law is not made for a righteous man, but for the lawless and disobedient, for the ungodly and for sinners, for unholy and profane, for murderers of fathers and murderers of mothers, for manslayers,

10. For whoremongers, for them that defile themselves with mankind, for menstealers, for liars, for perjured persons, and if there be any other thing that is contrary to sound doctrine;

11. According to the glorious gospel of the blessed God, which was committed to my trust.

12. And I thank Christ Jesus our Lord, who hath enabled me, for that he counted me faithful, putting me into the ministry;

13. Who was before a blasphemer, and a persecutor, and injurious: but I obtained mercy, because I did *it* ignorantly in unbelief.

14. And the grace of our Lord was exceeding abundant with faith and love which is in Christ Jesus.

15. This *is* a faithful saying, and worthy of all acceptation, that Christ Jesus came into the world to save sinners; of whom I am chief.

16. Howbeit for this cause I obtained mercy, that in me first Jesus Christ might show forth all long-suffering, for a pattern to them which should hereafter believe on him to life everlasting.

17. Now unto the King eternal, immortal, invisible, the only wise God, *be* honor and glory for ever and ever. Amen.

18. This charge I commit unto thee, son Timothy, according to the prophecies which went before on thee, that thou by them mightest war a good warfare;

19. Holding faith, and a good conscience; which some having put away, concerning faith have made shipwreck:

20. Of whom is Hy̆'mĕn-ē'ŭs and Alexander; whom I have delivered unto Satan, that they may learn not to blaspheme.

CHAPTER TWO

I exhort therefore, that, first of all, supplications, prayers, intercessions, *and* giving of thanks, be made for all men;

2. For kings, and *for* all that are in authority; that we may lead a quiet and peaceable life in all godliness and honesty.

3. For this *is* good and acceptable in the sight of God our Saviour;

4. Who will have all men to be saved, and to come unto the knowledge of the truth.

5. For *there is* one God, and one mediator between God and men, the man Christ Jesus;

6. Who gave himself a ransom for all, to be testified in due time.

7. Whereunto I am ordained a preacher, and an apostle, (I speak the truth in Christ, *and* lie not,) a teacher of the Gĕn'tīleṣ in faith and verity.

8. I will therefore that men pray every where, lifting up holy hands, without wrath and doubting.

9. In like manner also, that women adorn themselves in modest apparel, with shamefacedness and sobriety; not with braided hair, or gold, or pearls, or costly array;

10. But (which becometh women professing godliness) with good works.

11. Let the woman learn in silence with all subjection.

12. But I suffer not a woman to teach, nor to usurp authority over the man, but to be in silence.

13. For Adam was first formed, then Eve.

14. And Adam was not deceived, but the woman being deceived was in the transgression.

15. Notwithstanding she shall be saved in childbearing, if they continue in faith and charity and holiness with sobriety.

CHAPTER THREE

This *is* a true saying, If a man desire the office of a bishop, he desireth a good work.

2. A bishop then must be blameless, the husband of one wife, vigilant, sober, of good behavior, given to hospitality, apt to teach;

3. Not given to wine, no striker, not greedy of filthy lucre; but patient, not a brawler, not covetous;

4. One that ruleth well his own house, having his children in subjection with all gravity;

5. (For if a man know not how to rule his own house, how shall he take care of the church of God?)

6. Not a novice, lest being lifted up with pride he fall into the condemnation of the devil.

7. Moreover he must have a good report of them which are without; lest he fall into reproach and the snare of the devil.

8. Likewise *must* the deacons *be* grave, not double-tongued, not given to much wine, not greedy of filthy lucre;

9. Holding the mystery of the faith in a pure conscience.

10. And let these also first be proved; then let them use the office of a deacon, being *found* blameless.

11. Even so *must their* wives *be* grave, not slanderers, sober, faithful in all things.

12. Let the deacons be the husbands of one wife, ruling their children and their own houses well.

13. For they that have used the office of a deacon well purchase to themselves a good degree, and great boldness in the faith which is in Christ Jesus.

14. These things write I unto thee, hoping to come unto thee shortly:

15. But if I tarry long, that thou mayest know how thou oughtest to behave thyself in the house of God, which is the church of the living God, the pillar and ground of the truth.

16. And without controversy great is the mystery of godliness: God was manifest in the flesh, justified in the Spirit, seen of angels, preached unto the Gĕn'tīleș, believed on in the world, received up into glory.

CHAPTER FOUR

Now the Spirit speaketh expressly, that in the latter times some shall depart from the faith, giving heed to seducing spirits, and doctrines of devils;

2. Speaking lies in hypocrisy; having their conscience seared with a hot iron;

3. Forbidding to marry, *and commanding* to abstain from meats, which God hath created to be received with thanksgiving of them which believe and know the truth.

4. For every creature of God *is* good, and nothing to be refused, if it be received with thanksgiving:

5. For it is sanctified by the word of God and prayer.

6. If thou put the brethren in remembrance of these things, thou shalt be a good minister of Jesus Christ, nourished up in the words of faith and of good doctrine, whereunto thou hast attained.

7. But refuse profane and old wives' fables, and exercise thyself *rather* unto godliness.

8. For bodily exercise profiteth little: but godliness is profitable unto all things, having promise of the life that now is, and of that which is to come.

9. This *is* a faithful saying, and worthy of all acceptation.

10. For therefore we both labor and suffer reproach, because we trust in the living God, who is the Saviour of all men, specially of those that believe.

11. These things command and teach.

12. Let no man despise thy youth; but be thou an example of the believers, in word, in conversation, in charity, in spirit, in faith, in purity.

13. Till I come, give attendance to reading, to exhortation, to doctrine.

14. Neglect not the gift that is in thee, which was given thee by prophecy, with the laying on of the hands of the presbytery.

15. Meditate upon these things; give thyself wholly to them; that thy profiting may appear to all.

16. Take heed unto thyself, and unto the doctrine; continue in them: for in doing this thou shalt both save thyself, and them that hear thee.

CHAPTER FIVE

Rebuke not an elder, but entreat *him* as a father; *and* the younger men as brethren;

2. The elder women as mothers; the younger as sisters, with all purity.

3. Honor widows that are widows indeed.

4. But if any widow have children or nephews, let them learn first to show piety at home, and to requite their parents: for that is good and acceptable before God.

5. Now she that is a widow indeed, and desolate, trusteth in God, and continueth in supplications and prayers night and day.

6. But she that liveth in pleasure is dead while she liveth.

7. And these things give in charge, that they may be blameless.

8. But if any provide not for his own, and specially for those of his own house, he hath denied the faith, and is worse than an infidel.

9. Let not a widow be taken into the number under threescore years old, having been the wife of one man,

10. Well reported of for good works; if she have brought up children, if she have lodged strangers, if she have washed the saints' feet, if she have relieved the afflicted, if she have diligently followed every good work.

11. But the younger widows refuse: for when they have begun to wax wanton against Christ, they will marry;

12. Having damnation, because they have cast off their first faith.

13. And withal they learn *to be* idle, wandering about from house to house; and not only idle, but tattlers also and busybodies, speaking things which they ought not.

14. I will therefore that the younger women marry, bear children, guide the house, give none occasion to the adversary to speak reproachfully.

15. For some are already turned aside after Satan.

16. If any man or woman that believeth have widows, let them relieve them, and let not the church be charged; that it may relieve them that are widows indeed.

17. Let the elders that rule well be counted worthy of double honor, especially they who labor in the word and doctrine.

18. For the Scripture saith, Thou shalt not muzzle the ox that treadeth out the corn. And, The laborer *is* worthy of his reward.

19. Against an elder receive not an accusation, but before two or three witnesses.

20. Them that sin rebuke before all, that others also may fear.

21. I charge *thee* before God, and the Lord Jesus Christ, and the elect angels, that thou observe these things without preferring one before another, doing nothing by partiality.

22. Lay hands suddenly on no man, neither be partaker of other men's sins: keep thyself pure.

23. Drink no longer water, but use a little wine for thy stomach's sake and thine often infirmities.

24. Some men's sins are open beforehand, going before to judgment; and some *men* they follow after.

25. Likewise also the good works *of some* are manifest beforehand; and they that are otherwise cannot be hid.

CHAPTER SIX

Let as many servants as are under the yoke count their own masters worthy of all honor, that the name of God and *his* doctrine be not blasphemed.

2. And they that have believing masters, let them not despise *them*, because they are brethren; but rather do *them* service, because they are faithful and beloved, partakers of the benefit. These things teach and exhort.

3. If any man teach otherwise, and consent not to wholesome words, *even* the words of our Lord Jesus Christ, and to the doctrine which is according to godliness;

4. He is proud, knowing nothing, but doting about questions and strifes of words, whereof cometh envy, strife, railings, evil surmisings,

5. Perverse disputings of men of corrupt minds, and destitute of the truth, supposing that gain is godliness: from such withdraw thyself.

6. But godliness with contentment is great gain.

7. For we brought nothing into *this* world, *and it is* certain we can carry nothing out.

8. And having food and raiment; let us be therewith content.

9. But they that will be rich fall into temptation and a snare, and *into* many foolish and hurtful lusts, which drown men in destruction and perdition.

10. For the love of money is the root of all evil: which while some coveted after, they have erred from the faith, and pierced themselves through with many sorrows.

11. But thou, O man of God, flee these things; and follow after righteousness, godliness, faith, love, patience, meekness.

12. Fight the good fight of faith, lay hold on eternal life, whereunto thou art also called, and hast professed a good profession before many witnesses.

13. I give thee charge in the sight of God, who quickeneth all things, and *before* Christ Jesus, who before Pŏn'ṭĭ-ŭs Pilate witnessed a good confession;

14. That thou keep *this* commandment without spot, unrebukable, until the appearing of our Lord Jesus Christ:

15. Which in his times he shall show, *who is* the blessed and only Potentate, the King of kings, and Lord of lords;

16. Who only hath immortality, dwelling in the light which no man can approach unto; whom no man hath seen, nor can see: to whom *be* honor and power everlasting. Amen.

17. Charge them that are rich in this world, that they be not high-minded, nor trust in uncertain riches, but in the living God, who giveth us richly all things to enjoy;

18. That they do good, that they be rich in good works, ready to distribute, willing to communicate;

19. Laying up in store for themselves a good foundation against the time to come, that they may lay hold on eternal life.

20. O Timothy, keep that which is committed to thy trust, avoiding profane *and* vain babblings, and oppositions of science falsely so called:

21. Which some professing have erred concerning the faith. Grace *be* with thee. Amen.

2 TIMOTHY

CHAPTER ONE

Paul, an apostle of Jesus Christ by the will of God, according to the promise of life which is in Christ Jesus,

2. To Timothy, *my* dearly beloved son: Grace, mercy, *and* peace, from God the Father and Christ Jesus our Lord.

3. I thank God, whom I serve from *my* forefathers with pure conscience, that without ceasing I have remembrance of thee in my prayers night and day;

4. Greatly desiring to see thee, being mindful of thy tears, that I may be filled with joy;

5. When I call to remembrance the unfeigned faith that is in thee, which dwelt first in thy grandmother Lois, and thy mother Eunice; and I am persuaded that in thee also.

6. Wherefore I put thee in remembrance, that thou stir up the gift of God, which is in thee by the putting on of my hands.

7. For God hath not given us the spirit of fear; but of power, and of love, and of a sound mind.

8. Be not thou therefore ashamed of the testimony of our Lord, nor of me his prisoner: but be thou partaker of the afflictions of the gospel according to the power of God;

9. Who hath saved us, and called *us* with a holy calling, not according to our works, but according to his own purpose and grace, which was given us in Christ Jesus before the world began;

10. But is now made manifest by the appearing of our Saviour Jesus Christ, who hath abolished death, and hath brought life and immortality to light through the gospel:

11. Whereunto I am appointed a preacher, and an apostle, and a teacher of the Gĕn'tīleṣ.

12. For the which cause I also suffer these things: nevertheless I am not ashamed; for I know whom I have believed, and am persuaded that he is able to keep that which I have committed unto him against that day.

13. Hold fast the form of sound words, which thou hast heard of me, in faith and love which is in Christ Jesus.

14. That good thing which was committed unto thee keep by the Holy Ghost which dwelleth in us.

15. This thou knowest, that all they which are in Asia be turned away from me; of whom are Phȳ-ġĕl'lŭs and Hĕr-mŏġ'ē-nēs.

16. The Lord give mercy unto the house of Ŏn'ē-sĭph'ō-rŭs; for he oft refreshed me, and was not ashamed of my chain:

17. But, when he was in Rome, he sought me out very diligently, and found *me*.

18. The Lord grant unto him that he may find mercy of the Lord in that day: and in how many things he ministered unto me at Ĕph'ē-sŭs, thou knowest very well.

CHAPTER TWO

Thou therefore, my son, be strong in the grace that is in Christ Jesus.

2. And the things that thou hast heard of me among many witnesses, the same commit thou to faithful men, who shall be able to teach others also.

3. Thou therefore endure hardness, as a good soldier of Jesus Christ.

4. No man that warreth entangleth himself with the affairs of *this* life; that he may please him who hath chosen him to be a soldier.

5. And if a man also strive for masteries, *yet* is he not crowned, except he strive lawfully.

6. The husbandman that laboreth must be first partaker of the fruits.

7. Consider what I say; and the Lord give thee understanding in all things.

8. Remember that Jesus Christ of the seed of David was raised from the dead, according to my gospel:

9. Wherein I suffer trouble, as an evildoer, *even* unto bonds; but the word of God is not bound.

10. Therefore I endure all things for the elect's sake, that they may also obtain the salvation which is in Christ Jesus with eternal glory.

11. *It is* a faithful saying: For if we be dead with *him*, we shall also live with *him*:

12. If we suffer, we shall also reign with *him*: if we deny *him*, he also will deny us:

13. If we believe not, *yet* he abideth faithful: he cannot deny himself.

14. Of these things put *them* in remembrance, charging *them* before the Lord that they strive not about words to no profit, *but* to the subverting of the hearers.

15. Study to show thyself approved unto God, a workman that needeth not to be ashamed, rightly dividing the word of truth.

16. But shun profane *and* vain babblings: for they will increase unto more ungodliness.

17. And their word will eat as doth a canker: of whom is Hȳ'mĕn-ē'ŭs and Phĭ-lē'tŭs;

18. Who concerning the truth have erred, saying that the resurrection is past already; and overthrow the faith of some.

19. Nevertheless the foundation of God standeth sure, having this seal, The Lord knoweth them that are his. And, Let every one that nameth the name of Christ depart from iniquity.

20. But in a great house there are not only vessels of gold and of silver, but also of wood and of earth; and some to honor, and some to dishonor.

21. If a man therefore purge himself from these, he shall be a vessel unto honor, sanctified, and meet for the master's use, *and* prepared unto every good work.

22. Flee also youthful lusts: but follow righteousness, faith, charity, peace, with them that call on the Lord out of a pure heart.

23. But foolish and unlearned questions avoid, knowing that they do gender strifes.

24. And the servant of the Lord must not strive; but be gentle unto all *men*, apt to teach, patient;

25. In meekness instructing those that oppose themselves; if God peradventure will give them repentance to the acknowledging of the truth;

26. And *that* they may recover themselves out of the snare of the devil, who are taken captive by him at his will.

CHAPTER THREE

This know also, that in the last days perilous times shall come.

2. For men shall be lovers of their own selves, covetous, boasters, proud, blasphemers, disobedient to parents, unthankful, unholy,

3. Without natural affection, truce-breakers, false accusers, incontinent, fierce, despisers of those that are good,

4. Traitors, heady, high-minded, lovers of pleasures more than lovers of God;

5. Having a form of godliness, but denying the power thereof: from such turn away.

6. For of this sort are they which creep into houses, and lead captive silly women laden with sins, led away with divers lusts,

7. Ever learning, and never able to come to the knowledge of the truth.

8. Now as Jăn'nēṣ and Jăm'brēṣ withstood Moses, so do these also resist the truth: men of corrupt minds, reprobate concerning the faith.

9. But they shall proceed no further: for their folly shall be manifest unto all *men*, as theirs also was.

10. But thou hast fully known my doctrine, manner of life, purpose, faith, long-suffering, charity, patience,

11. Persecutions, afflictions, which came unto me at Ăn'tĭ-ŏ€h, at Ī-cō'nĭ-ŭm, at Lўs'trà; what persecutions I endured: but out of *them* all the Lord delivered me.

12. Yea, and all that will live godly in Christ Jesus shall suffer persecution.

13. But evil men and seducers shall wax worse and worse, deceiving, and being deceived.

14. But continue thou in the things which thou hast learned and hast been assured of, knowing of whom thou hast learned *them*;

15. And that from a child thou hast known the holy Scriptures, which are able to make thee wise unto salvation through faith which is in Christ Jesus.

16. All Scripture *is* given by inspiration of God, and *is* profitable for doctrine, for reproof, for correction, for instruction in righteousness:

17. That the man of God may be perfect, thoroughly furnished unto all good works.

CHAPTER FOUR

I charge *thee* therefore before God, and the Lord Jesus Christ, who shall judge the quick and the dead at his appearing and his kingdom;

2. Preach the word; be instant in season, out of season; reprove, rebuke, exhort with all long-suffering and doctrine.

3. For the time will come when they will not endure sound doctrine; but after their own lusts shall they heap to themselves teachers, having itching ears;

4. And they shall turn away *their* ears from the truth, and shall be turned unto fables.

5. But watch thou in all things, endure afflictions, do the work of an evangelist, make full proof of thy ministry.

6. For I am now ready to be offered, and the time of my departure is at hand.

7. I have fought a good fight, I have finished *my* course, I have kept the faith:

8. Henceforth there is laid up for me a crown of righteousness, which the Lord, the righteous judge, shall give me at that day: and not to me only, but unto all them also that love his appearing.

9. Do thy diligence to come shortly unto me:

10. For Dē'măs hath forsaken me, having loved this present world, and is departed unto Thĕs'sȧ-lō-nī'cȧ; Crĕs'çĕnṣ to Gȧ-lā'tĭ-ȧ; Titus unto Dăl-mā'tĭ-ȧ.

11. Only Luke is with me. Take Mark, and bring him with thee: for he is profitable to me for the ministry.

12. And Tў͏ҫh'ĭ-cŭs have I sent to Ĕph'ē-sŭs.

13. The cloak that I left at Trō'ăs with Carpus, when thou comest, bring *with thee*, and the books, *but* especially the parchments.

14. Alexander the coppersmith did me much evil: the Lord reward him according to his works:

15. Of whom be thou ware also; for he hath greatly withstood our words.

16. At my first answer no man stood with me, but all *men* forsook me: *I pray God* that it may not be laid to their charge.

17. Notwithstanding the Lord stood with me, and strengthened me; that by me the preaching might be fully known, and *that* all the Ġĕn'tīlĕṣ might hear: and I was delivered out of the mouth of the lion.

18. And the Lord shall deliver me from every evil work, and will preserve *me* unto his heavenly kingdom: to whom *be* glory for ever and ever. Amen.

19. Salute Prĭs'cà and Ăq'uĭ-là, and the household of Ŏn'ē-sĭph'ō-rŭs.

20. Ē-răs'tŭs abode at Corinth: but Trŏph'ĭ-mŭs have I left at Mī-lē'tŭm sick.

21. Do thy diligence to come before winter. Eū-bū'lŭs greeteth thee, and Pū'dĕnṣ, and Lī'nŭs, and Claudia, and all the brethren.

22. The Lord Jesus Christ *be* with thy spirit. Grace *be* with you. Amen.

TITUS

CHAPTER ONE

Paul, a servant of God, and an apostle of Jesus Christ, according to the faith of God's elect, and the acknowledging of the truth which is after godliness;

2. In hope of eternal life, which God, that cannot lie, promised before the world began;

3. But hath in due times manifested his word through preaching, which is committed unto me according to the commandment of God our Saviour;

4. To Titus, *mine* own son after the common faith: Grace, mercy, *and* peace, from God the Father and the Lord Jesus Christ our Saviour.

5. For this cause left I thee in Crete, that thou shouldest set in order the things that are wanting, and ordain elders in every city, as I had appointed thee:

6. If any be blameless, the husband of one wife, having faithful children not accused of riot or unruly.

7. For a bishop must be blameless, as the steward of God; not self-willed, not soon angry, not given to wine, no striker, not given to filthy lucre;

8. But a lover of hospitality, a lover of good men, sober, just, holy, temperate;

9. Holding fast the faithful word as he hath been taught, that he may be able by sound doctrine both to exhort and to convince the gainsayers.

10. For there are many unruly and vain talkers and deceivers, specially they of the circumcision:

11. Whose mouths must be stopped, who subvert whole houses, teaching things which they ought not, for filthy lucre's sake.

12. One of themselves, *even* a prophet of their own, said, The Crē'ţiăns̩ *are* always liars, evil beasts, slow bellies.

13. This witness is true. Wherefore rebuke them sharply, that they may be sound in the faith;

14. Not giving heed to Jewish fables, and commandments of men, that turn from the truth.

15. Unto the pure all things *are* pure: but unto them that are defiled and unbelieving *is* nothing pure; but even their mind and conscience is defiled.

16. They profess that they know God; but in works they deny *him*, being abominable, and disobedient, and unto every good work reprobate.

CHAPTER TWO

But speak thou the things which become sound doctrine:

2. That the aged men be sober, grave, temperate, sound in faith, in charity, in patience.

3. The aged women likewise, that *they be* in behavior as becometh holiness, not false accusers, not given to much wine, teachers of good things;

4. That they may teach the young women to be sober, to love their husbands, to love their children,

5. *To be* discreet, chaste, keepers at home, good, obedient to their own husbands, that the word of God be not blasphemed.

6. Young men likewise exhort to be sober minded.

7. In all things showing thyself a pattern of good works: in doctrine *showing* uncorruptness, gravity, sincerity,

8. Sound speech, that cannot be condemned; that he that is of the contrary part may be ashamed, having no evil thing to say of you.

9. *Exhort* servants to be obedient unto their own masters, *and* to please *them* well in all things; not answering again;

10. Not purloining, but showing all good fidelity; that they may adorn the doctrine of God our Saviour in all things.

11. For the grace of God that bringeth salvation hath appeared to all men,

12. Teaching us that, denying ungodliness and worldly lusts, we should live soberly, righteously, and godly, in this present world;

13. Looking for that blessed hope, and the glorious appearing of the great God and our Saviour Jesus Christ;

14. Who gave himself for us, that he might redeem us from all iniquity, and purify unto himself a peculiar people, zealous of good works.

15. These things speak, and exhort, and rebuke with all authority. Let no man despise thee.

CHAPTER THREE

Put them in mind to be subject to principalities and powers, to obey magistrates, to be ready to every good work,

2. To speak evil of no man, to be no brawlers, *but* gentle, showing all meekness unto all men.

3. For we ourselves also were sometime foolish, disobedient, deceived, serving divers lusts and pleasures, living in malice and envy, hateful, *and* hating one another.

4. But after that the kindness and love of God our Saviour toward man appeared,

5. Not by works of righteousness which we have done, but according to his mercy he saved us, by the washing of regeneration, and renewing of the Holy Ghost;

6. Which he shed on us abundantly through Jesus Christ our Saviour;

7. That being justified by his grace, we should be made heirs according to the hope of eternal life.

8. *This is* a faithful saying, and these things I will that thou affirm constantly, that they which have believed in God might be careful to maintain good works. These things are good and profitable unto men.

9. But avoid foolish questions, and genealogies, and contentions, and strivings about the law; for they are unprofitable and vain.

10. A man that is a heretic, after the first and second admonition, reject;

11. Knowing that he that is such is subverted, and sinneth, being condemned of himself.

12. When I shall send Är'tē-măs unto thee, or Tўєh'ĭ-cŭs, be diligent to come unto me to Nī-cŏp'ō-lĭs: for I have determined there to winter.

13. Bring Zē'nås the lawyer and Ả-pŏl'lŏs on their journey diligently, that nothing be wanting unto them.

14. And let ours also learn to maintain good works for necessary uses, that they be not unfruitful.

15. All that are with me salute thee. Greet them that love us in the faith. Grace *be* with you all. Amen.

HEBREWS

CHAPTER ONE

God, who at sundry times and in divers manners spake in time past unto the fathers by the prophets,

2. Hath in these last days spoken unto us by *his* Son, whom he hath appointed heir of all things, by whom also he made the worlds;

3. Who being the brightness of *his* glory, and the express image of his person, and upholding all things by the word of his power, when he had by himself purged our sins, sat down on the right hand of the Majesty on high;

4. Being made so much better than the angels, as he hath by inheritance obtained a more excellent name than they.

5. For unto which of the angels said he at any time, Thou art my Son, this day have I begotten thee? And again, I will be to him a Father, and he shall be to me a Son?

6. And again, when he bringeth in the first-begotten into the world, he saith, And let all the angels of God worship him.

7. And of the angels he saith, Who maketh his angels spirits, and his ministers a flame of fire.

8. But unto the Son *he saith*, Thy throne, O God, *is* for ever and ever: a sceptre of righteousness *is* the sceptre of thy kingdom.

9. Thou hast loved righteousness, and hated iniquity; therefore God, *even* thy God, hath anointed thee with the oil of gladness above thy fellows.

10. And, Thou, Lord, in the beginning hast laid the foundation of the earth; and the heavens are the works of thine hands.

11. They shall perish, but thou remainest: and they all shall wax old as doth a garment;

12. And as a vesture shalt thou fold them up, and they shall be changed: but thou art the same, and thy years shall not fail.

13. But to which of the angels said he at any time, Sit on my right hand, until I make thine enemies thy footstool?

14. Are they not all ministering spirits, sent forth to minister for them who shall be heirs of salvation?

CHAPTER TWO

Therefore we ought to give the more earnest heed to the things which we have heard, lest at any time we should let *them* slip.

2. For if the word spoken by angels was steadfast, and every transgression and disobedience received a just recompense of reward;

3. How shall we escape, if we neglect so great salvation; which at the first began to be spoken by the Lord, and was confirmed unto us by them that heard *him*;

4. God also bearing *them* witness, both with signs and wonders, and with divers miracles, and gifts of the Holy Ghost, according to his own will?

5. For unto the angels hath he not put in subjection the world to come, whereof we speak.

6. But one in a certain place testified, saying, What is man, that thou art mindful of him? or the son of man, that thou visitest him?

7. Thou madest him a little lower than the angels; thou crownedst him with glory and honor, and didst set him over the works of thy hands:

8. Thou hast put all things in subjection under his feet. For in that he put all in subjection under him, he left nothing *that is* not put under him. But now we see not yet all things put under him.

9. But we see Jesus, who was made a little lower than the angels for the suffering of death, crowned with glory and honor; that he by the grace of God should taste death for every man.

10. For it became him, for whom *are* all things, and by whom *are* all things, in bringing many sons unto glory, to make the captain of their salvation perfect through sufferings.

11. For both he that sanctifieth and they who are sanctified *are* all of one: for which cause he is not ashamed to call them brethren,

12. Saying, I will declare thy name unto my brethren, in the midst of the church will I sing praise unto thee.

13. And again, I will put my trust in him. And again, Behold I and the children which God hath given me.

14. Forasmuch then as the children are partakers of flesh and blood, he also himself likewise took part of the same; that through death he might destroy him that had the power of death, that is, the devil;

15. And deliver them, who through fear of death were all their lifetime subject to bondage.

16. For verily he took not on *him the nature of* angels; but he took on *him* the seed of Abraham.

17. Wherefore in all things it behooved him to be made like unto *his* brethren, that he might be a merciful and faithful high priest in things *pertaining* to God, to make reconciliation for the sins of the people.

18. For in that he himself hath suffered being tempted, he is able to succor them that are tempted.

CHAPTER THREE

Wherefore, holy brethren, partakers of the heavenly calling, consider the Apostle and High Priest of our profession, Christ Jesus;

2. Who was faithful to him that appointed him, as also Moses *was faithful* in all his house.

3. For this *man* was counted worthy of more glory than Moses, inasmuch as he who hath builded the house hath more honor than the house.

4. For every house is builded by some *man*; but he that built all things *is* God.

5. And Moses verily *was* faithful in all his house as a servant, for a testimony of those things which were to be spoken after;

6. But Christ as a son over his own house; whose house are we, if we hold fast the confidence and the rejoicing of the hope firm unto the end.

7. Wherefore as the Holy Ghost saith, To-day if ye will hear his voice,

8. Harden not your hearts, as in the provocation, in the day of temptation in the wilderness:

9. When your fathers tempted me, proved me, and saw my works forty years.

10. Wherefore I was grieved with that generation, and said, They do always err in *their* heart; and they have not known my ways.

11. So I sware in my wrath, They shall not enter into my rest.

12. Take heed, brethren, lest there be in any of you an evil heart of unbelief, in departing from the living God.

13. But exhort one another daily, while it is called To-day; lest any of you be hardened through the deceitfulness of sin.

14. For we are made partakers of Christ, if we hold the beginning of our confidence steadfast unto the end;

15. While it is said, To-day if ye will hear his voice, harden not your hearts, as in the provocation.

16. For some, when they had heard, did provoke: howbeit not all that came out of Egypt by Moses.

17. But with whom was he grieved forty years? *was it* not with them that had sinned, whose carcasses fell in the wilderness?

18. And to whom sware he that they should not enter into his rest, but to them that believed not?

19. So we see that they could not enter in because of unbelief.

CHAPTER FOUR

Let us therefore fear, lest, a promise being left *us* of entering into his rest, any of you should seem to come short of it.

2. For unto us was the gospel preached, as well as unto them: but the word preached did not profit them, not being mixed with faith in them that heard *it*.

3. For we which have believed do enter into rest, as he said, As I have sworn in my wrath, if they shall enter into my rest: although the works were finished from the foundation of the world.

4. For he spake in a certain place of the seventh *day* on this wise, And God did rest the seventh day from all his works.

5. And in this *place* again, If they shall enter into my rest.

6. Seeing therefore it remaineth that some must enter therein, and they to whom it was first preached entered not in because of unbelief:

7. Again, he limiteth a certain day, saying in David, To-day, after so long a time; as it is said, To-day if ye will hear his voice, harden not your hearts.

8. For if Jesus had given them rest, then would he not afterward have spoken of another day.

9. There remaineth therefore a rest to the people of God.

10. For he that is entered into his rest, he also hath ceased from his own works, as God *did* from his.

11. Let us labor therefore to enter into that rest, lest any man fall after the same example of unbelief.

12. For the word of God *is* quick, and powerful, and sharper than any two-edged sword, piercing even to the dividing asunder of soul and spirit, and of the joints and marrow, and *is* a discerner of the thoughts and intents of the heart.

13. Neither is there any creature that is not manifest in his sight: but all things *are* naked and opened unto the eyes of him with whom we have to do.

14. Seeing then that we have a great high priest, that is passed into the heavens, Jesus the Son of God, let us hold fast *our* profession.

15. For we have not a high priest which cannot be touched with the feeling of our infirmities; but was in all points tempted like as *we are, yet* without sin.

16. Let us therefore come boldly unto the throne of grace, that we may obtain mercy, and find grace to help in time of need.

CHAPTER FIVE

For every high priest taken from among men is ordained for men in things *pertaining* to God, that he may offer both gifts and sacrifices for sins:

2. Who can have compassion on the ignorant, and on them that are out of the way; for that he himself also is compassed with infirmity.

3. And by reason hereof he ought, as for the people, so also for himself, to offer for sins.

4. And no man taketh this honor unto himself, but he that is called of God, as *was* Aaron.

5. So also Christ glorified not himself to be made a high priest; but he that said unto him, Thou art my Son, to-day have I begotten thee.

6. As he saith also in another *place*, Thou *art* a priest for ever after the order of Mĕl-ϲhĭṣ'ē-dĕc.

7. Who in the days of his flesh, when he had offered up prayers and supplications with strong crying and tears unto him that was able to save him from death, and was heard in that he feared;

8. Though he were a Son, yet learned he obedience by the things which he suffered;

9. And being made perfect, he became the author of eternal salvation unto all them that obey him;

10. Called of God a high priest after the order of Mĕl-ϲhĭṣ'ē-dĕc.

11. Of whom we have many things to say, and hard to be uttered, seeing ye are dull of hearing.

12. For when for the time ye ought to be teachers, ye have need that one teach you again which *be* the first principles of the oracles of God; and are become such as have need of milk, and not of strong meat.

13. For every one that useth milk *is* unskilful in the word of righteousness: for he is a babe.

14. But strong meat belongeth to them that are of full age, *even* those who by reason of use have their senses exercised to discern both good and evil.

CHAPTER SIX

Therefore leaving the principles of the doctrine of Christ, let us go on unto perfection; not laying again the foundation of repentance from dead works, and of faith toward God,

2. Of the doctrine of baptisms, and of laying on of hands, and of resurrection of the dead, and of eternal judgment.

3. And this will we do, if God permit.

4. For *it is* impossible for those who were once enlightened, and have tasted of the heavenly gift, and were made partakers of the Holy Ghost,

5. And have tasted the good word of God, and the powers of the world to come,

6. If they shall fall away, to renew them again unto repentance; seeing they crucify to themselves the Son of God afresh, and put *him* to an open shame.

7. For the earth which drinketh in the rain that cometh oft upon it, and bringeth forth herbs meet for them by whom it is dressed, receiveth blessing from God:

8. But that which beareth thorns and briers *is* rejected, and *is* nigh unto cursing; whose end *is* to be burned.

9. But, beloved, we are persuaded better things of you, and things that accompany salvation, though we thus speak.

10. For God *is* not unrighteous to forget your work and labor of love, which ye have showed toward his name, in that ye have ministered to the saints, and do minister.

11. And we desire that every one of you do show the same diligence to the full assurance of hope unto the end:

12. That ye be not slothful, but followers of them who through faith and patience inherit the promises.

13. For when God made promise to Abraham, because he could swear by no greater, he sware by himself,

14. Saying, Surely blessing I will bless thee, and multiplying I will multiply thee.

15. And so, after he had patiently endured, he obtained the promise.

16. For men verily swear by the greater: and an oath for confirmation *is* to them an end of all strife.

17. Wherein God, willing more abundantly to show unto the heirs of promise the immutability of his counsel, confirmed *it* by an oath:

18. That by two immutable things, in which *it was* impossible for God to lie, we might have a strong consolation, who have fled for refuge to lay hold upon the hope set before us:

19. Which *hope* we have as an anchor of the soul, both sure and steadfast, and which entereth into that within the veil;

20. Whither the forerunner is for us entered, *even* Jesus, made a high priest for ever after the order of Měl-ϵhĭṣ'ē-dēc.

CHAPTER SEVEN

For this Měl-ϵhĭṣ'e-děc, king of Sā'lěm, priest of the most high God, who met Abraham returning from the slaughter of the kings, and blessed him;

2. To whom also Abraham gave a tenth part of all; first being by interpretation King of righteousness, and after that also King of Sā'lěm, which is, King of peace;

3. Without father, without mother, without descent, having neither beginning of days, nor end of life; but made like unto the Son of God; abideth a priest continually.

4. Now consider how great this man *was*, unto whom even the patriarch Abraham gave the tenth of the spoils.

5. And verily they that are of the sons of Levi, who receive the office of the priesthood, have a commandment to take tithes of the people according to the law, that is, of their brethren, though they come out of the loins of Abraham:

6. But he whose descent is not counted from them received tithes of Abraham, and blessed him that had the promises.

7. And without all contradiction the less is blessed of the better.

8. And here men that die receive tithes; but there he *receiveth them*, of whom it is witnessed that he liveth.

9. And as I may so say, Levi also, who receiveth tithes, paid tithes in Abraham.

10. For he was yet in the loins of his father, when Měl-ϵhĭṣ’ē-děc met him.

11. If therefore perfection were by the Lē-vĭt’ĭ-căl priesthood, (for under it the people received the law,) what further need *was there* that another priest should rise after the order of Mělϵhĭṣ’ē-děc, and not be called after the order of Aaron?

12. For the priesthood being changed, there is made of necessity a change also of the law.

13. For he of whom these things are spoken pertaineth to another tribe, of which no man gave attendance at the altar.

14. For *it is* evident that our Lord sprang out of Jṳ'dȧ; of which tribe Moses spake nothing concerning priesthood.

15. And it is yet far more evident: for that after the similitude of Mĕl-ϵhĭṣ'ē-dēc there ariseth another priest,

16. Who is made, not after the law of a carnal commandment, but after the power of an endless life.

17. For he testifieth, Thou *art* a priest for ever after the order of Mĕlϵhĭṣ'ē-dēc.

18. For there is verily a disannulling of the commandment going before for the weakness and unprofitableness thereof.

19. For the law made nothing perfect, but the bringing in of a better hope *did*; by the which we draw nigh unto God.

20. And inasmuch as not without an oath *he was made priest*:

21. (For those priests were made without an oath; but this with an oath by him that said unto him, The Lord sware and will not repent, Thou *art* a priest for ever after the order of Mĕl-ϵhĭṣ'ē-dēc:)

22. By so much was Jesus made a surety of a better testament.

23. And they truly were many priests, because they were not suffered to continue by reason of death:

24. But this *man*, because he continueth ever, hath an unchangeable priesthood.

25. Wherefore he is able also to save them to the uttermost that come unto God by him, seeing he ever liveth to make intercession for them.

26. For such a high priest became us, *who is* holy, harmless, undefiled, separate from sinners, and made higher than the heavens;

27. Who needeth not daily, as those high priests, to offer up sacrifice, first for his own sins, and then for the people's: for this he did once, when he offered up himself.

28. For the law maketh men high priests which have infirmity; but the word of the oath, which was since the law, *maketh* the Son, who is consecrated for evermore.

CHAPTER EIGHT

Now of the things which we have spoken *this is* the sum: We have such a high priest, who is set on the right hand of the throne of the Majesty in the heavens;

2. A minister of the sanctuary, and of the true tabernacle, which the Lord pitched, and not man.

3. For every high priest is ordained to offer gifts and sacrifices: wherefore *it is* of necessity that this man have somewhat also to offer.

4. For if he were on earth, he should not be a priest, seeing that there are priests that offer gifts according to the law:

5. Who serve unto the example and shadow of heavenly things, as Moses was admonished of God when he was about to make the tabernacle: for, See, saith he, *that* thou make all things according to the pattern showed to thee in the mount.

6. But now hath he obtained a more excellent ministry, by how much also he is the mediator of a better covenant, which was established upon better promises.

7. For if that first *covenant* had been faultless, then should no place have been sought for the second.

8. For finding fault with them, he saith, Behold, the days come, saith the Lord, when I will make a new covenant with the house of Ĭṣ'rā-ĕl and with the house of Judah:

9. Not according to the covenant that I made with their fathers, in the day when I took them by the hand to lead them out of the land of Egypt; because they continued not in my covenant, and I regarded them not, saith the Lord.

10. For this *is* the covenant that I will make with the house of Ĭṣ'rā-ĕl after those days, saith the Lord; I will put my laws into their mind, and write them in their hearts: and I will be to them a God, and they shall be to me a people:

11. And they shall not teach every man his neighbor, and every man his brother, saying, Know the Lord: for all shall know me, from the least to the greatest.

12. For I will be merciful to their unrighteousness, and their sins and their iniquities will I remember no more.

13. In that he saith, A new *covenant*, he hath made the first old. Now that which decayeth and waxeth old *is* ready to vanish away.

CHAPTER NINE

Then verily the first *covenant* had also ordinances of divine service, and a worldly sanctuary.

2. For there was a tabernacle made; the first, wherein *was* the candlestick, and the table, and the showbread; which is called the sanctuary.

3. And after the second veil, the tabernacle which is called the holiest of all;

4. Which had the golden censer, and the ark of the covenant overlaid round about with gold, wherein *was* the golden pot that had manna, and Aaron's rod that budded, and the tables of the covenant;

5. And over it the cherubim of glory shadowing the mercy seat; of which we cannot now speak particularly.

6. Now when these things were thus ordained, the priests went always into the first tabernacle, accomplishing the service *of God*.

7. But into the second *went* the high priest alone once every year, not without blood, which he offered for himself, and *for* the errors of the people:

8. The Holy Ghost this signifying, that the way into the holiest of all was not yet made manifest, while as the first tabernacle was yet standing:

9. Which *was* a figure for the time then present, in which were offered both gifts and sacrifices, that could not make him that did the service perfect, as pertaining to the conscience;

10. *Which stood* only in meats and drinks, and divers washings, and carnal ordinances, imposed *on them* until the time of reformation.

11. But Christ being come a high priest of good things to come, by a greater and more perfect tabernacle, not made with hands, that is to say, not of this building;

12. Neither by the blood of goats and calves, but by his own blood he entered in once into the holy place, having obtained eternal redemption *for us*.

13. For if the blood of bulls and of goats, and the ashes of a heifer sprinkling the unclean, sanctifieth to the purifying of the flesh;

14. How much more shall the blood of Christ, who through the eternal Spirit offered himself without spot to God, purge your conscience from dead works to serve the living God?

15. And for this cause he is the mediator of the new testament, that by means of death, for the redemption of the transgressions *that were* under the first testament, they which are called might receive the promise of eternal inheritance.

16. For where a testament *is*, there must also of necessity be the death of the testator.

17. For a testament *is* of force after men are dead: otherwise it is of no strength at all while the testator liveth.

18. Whereupon neither the first *testament* was dedicated without blood.

19. For when Moses had spoken every precept to all the people according to the law, he took the blood of calves and of goats, with water, and scarlet wool, and hyssop, and sprinkled both the book and all the people,

20. Saying, This *is* the blood of the testament which God hath enjoined unto you.

21. Moreover he sprinkled likewise with blood both the tabernacle, and all the vessels of the ministry.

22. And almost all things are by the law purged with blood; and without shedding of blood is no remission.

23. *It was* therefore necessary that the patterns of things in the heavens should be purified with these; but the heavenly things themselves with better sacrifices than these.

24. For Christ is not entered into the holy places made with hands, *which are* the figures of the true; but into heaven itself, now to appear in the presence of God for us:

25. Nor yet that he should offer himself often, as the high priest entereth into the holy place every year with blood of others;

26. For then must he often have suffered since the foundation of the world: but now once in the end of the world hath he appeared to put away sin by the sacrifice of himself.

27. And as it is appointed unto men once to die, but after this the judgment:

28. So Christ was once offered to bear the sins of many; and unto them that look for him shall he appear the second time without sin unto salvation.

CHAPTER TEN

For the law having a shadow of good things to come, *and* not the very image of the things, can never with those sacrifices, which they offered year by year continually, make the comers thereunto perfect.

2. For then would they not have ceased to be offered? because that the worshippers once purged should have had no more conscience of sins.

3. But in those *sacrifices there is* a remembrance again *made* of sins every year.

4. For *it is* not possible that the blood of bulls and of goats should take away sins.

5. Wherefore, when he cometh into the world, he saith, Sacrifice and offering thou wouldest not, but a body hast thou prepared me:

6. In burnt offerings and *sacrifices* for sin thou hast had no pleasure.

7. Then said I, Lo, I come (in the volume of the book it is written of me) to do thy will, O God.

8. Above when he said, Sacrifice and offering and burnt offerings and *offering* for sin thou wouldest not, neither hadst pleasure *therein*: which are offered by the law;

9. Then said he, Lo, I come to do thy will, O God. He taketh away the first, that he may establish the second.

10. By the which will we are sanctified through the offering of the body of Jesus Christ once *for all*.

11. And every priest standeth daily ministering and offering oftentimes the same sacrifices, which can never take away sins:

12. But this man, after he had offered one sacrifice for sins for ever, sat down on the right hand of God;

13. From henceforth expecting till his enemies be made his footstool.

14. For by one offering he hath perfected for ever them that are sanctified.

15. *Whereof* the Holy Ghost also is a witness to us: for after that he had said before,

16. This *is* the covenant that I will make with them after those days, saith the Lord; I will put my laws into their hearts, and in their minds will I write them;

17. And their sins and iniquities will I remember no more.

18. Now where remission of these *is, there is* no more offering for sin.

19. Having therefore, brethren, boldness to enter into the holiest by the blood of Jesus,

20. By a new and living way, which he hath consecrated for us, through the veil, that is to say, his flesh;

21. And *having* a high priest over the house of God;

22. Let us draw near with a true heart in full assurance of faith, having our hearts sprinkled from an evil conscience, and our bodies washed with pure water.

23. Let us hold fast the profession of *our* faith without wavering; for he *is* faithful that promised;

24. And let us consider one another to provoke unto love and to good works:

25. Not forsaking the assembling of ourselves together, as the manner of some *is;* but exhorting *one another:* and so much the more, as ye see the day approaching.

26. For if we sin wilfully after that we have received the knowledge of the truth, there remaineth no more sacrifice for sins,

27. But a certain fearful looking for of judgment and fiery indignation, which shall devour the adversaries.

28. He that despised Moses' law died without mercy under two or three witnesses:

29. Of how much sorer punishment, suppose ye, shall he be thought worthy, who hath trodden under foot the Son of God, and hath counted the blood of the covenant, wherewith he was sanctified, an unholy thing, and hath done despite unto the Spirit of grace?

30. For we know him that hath said, Vengeance *belongeth* unto me, I will recompense, saith the Lord. And again, The Lord shall judge his people.

31. *It is* a fearful thing to fall into the hands of the living God.

32. But call to remembrance the former days, in which, after ye were illuminated, ye endured a great fight of afflictions;

33. Partly, whilst ye were made a gazingstock both by reproaches and afflictions; and partly, whilst ye became companions of them that were so used.

34. For ye had compassion of me in my bonds, and took joyfully the spoiling of your goods, knowing in yourselves that ye have in heaven a better and an enduring substance.

35. Cast not away therefore your confidence, which hath great recompense of reward.

36. For ye have need of patience, that, after ye have done the will of God, ye might receive the promise.

37. For yet a little while, and he that shall come will come, and will not tarry.

38. Now the just shall live by faith: but if *any man* draw back, my soul shall have no pleasure in him.

39. But we are not of them who draw back unto perdition; but of them that believe to the saving of the soul.

CHAPTER ELEVEN

Now faith is the substance of things hoped for, the evidence of things not seen.

2. For by it the elders obtained a good report.

3. Through faith we understand that the worlds were framed by the word of God, so that things which are seen were not made of things which do appear.

4. By faith Abel offered unto God a more excellent sacrifice than Cain, by which he obtained witness that he was righteous, God testifying of his gifts: and by it he being dead yet speaketh.

5. By faith Enoch was translated that he should not see death; and was not found, because God had translated him: for before his translation he had this testimony, that he pleased God.

6. But without faith *it is* impossible to please *him:* for he that cometh to God must believe that he is, and *that* he is a rewarder of them that diligently seek him.

7. By faith Noah, being warned of God of things not seen as yet, moved with fear, prepared an ark to the saving of his house; by the which he condemned the world, and became heir of the righteousness which is by faith.

8. By faith Abraham, when he was called to go out into a place which he should after receive for an inheritance, obeyed; and he went out, not knowing whither he went.

9. By faith he sojourned in the land of promise, as *in* a strange country, dwelling in tabernacles with Isaac and Jacob, the heirs with him of the same promise:

10. For he looked for a city which hath foundations, whose builder and maker *is* God.

11. Through faith also Sarah herself received strength to conceive seed, and was delivered of a child when she was past age, because she judged him faithful who had promised.

12. Therefore sprang there even of one, and him as good as dead, *so many* as the stars of the sky in multitude, and as the sand which is by the seashore innumerable.

13. These all died in faith, not having received the promises, but having seen them afar off, and were persuaded of *them*, and embraced *them*, and confessed that they were strangers and pilgrims on the earth.

14. For they that say such things declare plainly that they seek a country.

15. And truly, if they had been mindful of that *country* from whence they came out, they might have had opportunity to have returned.

16. But now they desire a better *country*, that is, a heavenly: wherefore God is not ashamed to be called their God: for he hath prepared for them a city.

17. By faith Abraham, when he was tried, offered up Isaac: and he that had received the promises offered up his only begotten *son*,

18. Of whom it was said, That in Isaac shall thy seed be called:

19. Accounting that God *was* able to raise *him* up, even from the dead; from whence also he received him in a figure.

20. By faith Isaac blessed Jacob and Ē′sáū concerning things to come.

21. By faith Jacob, when he was a dying, blessed both the sons of Joseph; and worshipped, *leaning* upon the top of his staff.

22. By faith Joseph, when he died, made mention of the departing of the children of Ĭṣ′rā-ĕl; and gave command-ment concerning his bones.

23. By faith Moses, when he was born, was hid three months of his parents, because they saw *he was* a proper child; and they were not afraid of the king's commandment.

24. By faith Moses, when he was come to years, refused to be called the son of Phā′raōh's daughter;

25. Choosing rather to suffer affliction with the people of God, than to enjoy the pleasures of sin for a season;

26. Esteeming the reproach of Christ greater riches than the treasures in Egypt: for he had respect unto the recompense of the reward.

27. By faith he forsook Egypt, not fearing the wrath of the king: for he endured, as seeing him who is invisible.

28. Through faith he kept the passover, and the sprinkling of blood, lest he that destroyed the firstborn should touch them.

29. By faith they passed through the Red sea as by dry *land:* which the Egyptians assaying to do were drowned.

30. By faith the walls of Jĕr'ĭ-ɛhō fell down, after they were compassed about seven days.

31. By faith the harlot Rā'hăb perished not with them that believed not, when she had received the spies with peace.

32. And what shall I more say? for the time would fail me to tell of Gideon, and *of* Bā'răk, and *of* Samson, and *of* Jĕph'thàh; *of* David also, and Samuel, and *of* the prophets:

33. Who through faith subdued kingdoms, wrought righteousness, obtained promises, stopped the mouths of lions,

34. Quenched the violence of fire, escaped the edge of the sword, out of weakness were made strong, waxed valiant in fight, turned to flight the armies of the aliens.

35. Women received their dead raised to life again: and others were tortured, not accepting deliverance; that they might obtain a better resurrection:

36. And others had trial of *cruel* mockings and scourgings, yea, moreover of bonds and imprisonment:

37. They were stoned, they were sawn asunder, were tempted, were slain with the sword: they wandered about in sheepskins and goatskins; being destitute, afflicted, tormented;

38. Of whom the world was not worthy: they wandered in deserts, and *in* mountains, and *in* dens and caves of the earth.

39. And these all, having obtained a good report through faith, received not the promise:

40. God having provided some better thing for us, that they without us should not be made perfect.

CHAPTER TWELVE

Wherefore, seeing we also are compassed about with so great a cloud of witnesses, let us lay aside every weight, and the sin which doth so easily beset *us*, and let us run with patience the race that is set before us,

2. Looking unto Jesus the author and finisher of *our* faith; who for the joy that was set before him endured the cross, despising the shame, and is set down at the right hand of the throne of God.

3. For consider him that endured such contradiction of sinners against himself, lest ye be wearied and faint in your minds.

4. Ye have not yet resisted unto blood, striving against sin.

5. And ye have forgotten the exhortation which speaketh unto you as unto children, My son, despise not thou the chastening of the Lord, nor faint when thou art rebuked of him:

6. For whom the Lord loveth he chasteneth, and scourgeth every son whom he receiveth.

7. If ye endure chastening, God dealeth with you as with sons; for what son is he whom the father chasteneth not?

8. But if ye be without chastisement, whereof all are par-takers, then are ye bastards, and not sons.

9. Furthermore, we have had fathers of our flesh which corrected *us*, and we gave *them* reverence: shall we not much rather be in subjection unto the Father of spirits, and live?

10. For they verily for a few days chastened *us* after their own pleasure; but he for *our* profit, that *we* might be par-takers of his holiness.

11. Now no chastening for the present seemeth to be joy-ous, but grievous: nevertheless, afterward it yieldeth the peaceable fruit of righteousness unto them which are exer-cised thereby.

12. Wherefore lift up the hands which hang down, and the feeble knees;

13. And make straight paths for your feet, lest that which is lame be turned out of the way; but let it rather be healed.

14. Follow peace with all *men*, and holiness, without which no man shall see the Lord:

15. Looking diligently lest any man fail of the grace of God; lest any root of bitterness springing up trouble *you*, and thereby many be defiled;

16. Lest there *be* any fornicator, or profane person, as Ē'saū, who for one morsel of meat sold his birthright.

17. For ye know how that afterward, when he would have inherited the blessing, he was rejected: for he found no place of repentance, though he sought it carefully with tears.

18. For ye are not come unto the mount that might be touched, and that burned with fire, nor unto blackness, and darkness, and tempest,

19. And the sound of a trumpet, and the voice of words; which *voice* they that heard entreated that the word should not be spoken to them any more:

20. (For they could not endure that which was commanded, And if so much as a beast touch the mountain, it shall be stoned, or thrust through with a dart:

21. And so terrible was the sight, *that* Moses said, I exceedingly fear and quake:)

22. But ye are come unto mount Sī'ŏn, and unto the city of the living God, the heavenly Jerusalem, and to an innumerable company of angels,

23. To the general assembly and church of the firstborn, which are written in heaven, and to God the Judge of all, and to the spirits of just men made perfect,

24. And to Jesus the mediator of the new covenant, and to the blood of sprinkling, that speaketh better things than *that of* Abel.

25. See that ye refuse not him that speaketh: for if they escaped not who refused him that spake on earth, much more *shall not* we *escape*, if we turn away from him that *speaketh* from heaven:

26. Whose voice then shook the earth: but now he hath promised, saying, Yet once more I shake not the earth only, but also heaven.

27. And this *word*, Yet once more, signifieth the removing of those things that are shaken, as of things that are made, that those things which cannot be shaken may remain.

28. Wherefore we receiving a kingdom which cannot be moved, let us have grace, whereby we may serve God acceptably with reverence and godly fear:

29. For our God *is* a consuming fire.

CHAPTER THIRTEEN

Let brotherly love continue.

2. Be not forgetful to entertain strangers: for thereby some have entertained angels unawares.

3. Remember them that are in bonds, as bound with them; *and* them which suffer adversity, as being yourselves also in the body.

4. Marriage *is* honorable in all, and the bed undefiled: but whoremongers and adulterers God will judge.

5. *Let your* conversation *be* without covetousness; *and be* content with such things as ye have: for he hath said, I will never leave thee, nor forsake thee.

6. So that we may boldly say, The Lord *is* my helper, and I will not fear what man shall do unto me.

7. Remember them which have the rule over you, who have spoken unto you the word of God: whose faith follow, considering the end of *their* conversation.

8. Jesus Christ the same yesterday, and to-day, and for ever.

9. Be not carried about with divers and strange doctrines: for *it is* a good thing that the heart be established with grace; not with meats, which have not profited them that have been occupied therein.

10. We have an altar, whereof they have no right to eat which serve the tabernacle.

11. For the bodies of those beasts, whose blood is brought into the sanctuary by the high priest for sin, are burned without the camp.

12. Wherefore Jesus also, that he might sanctify the people with his own blood, suffered without the gate.

13. Let us go forth therefore unto him without the camp, bearing his reproach.

14. For here have we no continuing city, but we seek one to come.

15. By him therefore let us offer the sacrifice of praise to God continually, that is, the fruit of *our* lips, giving thanks to his name.

16. But to do good and to communicate forget not: for with such sacrifices God is well pleased.

17. Obey them that have the rule over you, and submit yourselves: for they watch for your souls, as they that must give account, that they may do it with joy, and not with grief: for that *is* unprofitable for you.

18. Pray for us: for we trust we have a good conscience, in all things willing to live honestly.

19. But I beseech *you* the rather to do this, that I may be restored to you the sooner.

20. Now the God of peace, that brought again from the dead our Lord Jesus, that great shepherd of the sheep, through the blood of the everlasting covenant,

21. Make you perfect in every good work to do his will, working in you that which is well-pleasing in his sight, through Jesus Christ; to whom *be* glory for ever and ever. Amen.

22. And I beseech you, brethren, suffer the word of exhortation: for I have written a letter unto you in few words.

23. Know ye that *our* brother Timothy is set at liberty; with whom, if he come shortly, I will see you.

24. Salute all them that have the rule over you, and all the saints. They of Italy salute you.

25. Grace *be* with you all. Amen.

John Shelby Spong is the Episcopal Bishop of Newark and author of *Rescuing the Bible from Fundamentalism, Born of a Woman, Liberating the Gospels,* and *Why Christianity Must Change or Die.*